KNIT
Christmas Stockings

19 PATTERNS FOR STOCKINGS & ORNAMENTS

Edited by ~~~~~~~~~~

Storey Publishing

*The mission of Storey Publishing is to serve our customers by
publishing practical information that encourages
personal independence in harmony with the environment.*

Edited by Gwen W. Steege
Art direction and book design by Jessica Armstrong

Cover and interior photography by © Geneve Hoffman, except for page 77 by Mars Vilaubi
Illustrations by Alison Kolesar
Charts by Jen Rork

Indexed by Christine R. Lindemer, Boston Road Communications

Storey Publishing
210 MASS MoCA Way
North Adams, MA 01247
www.storey.com

Printed in China by Shenzhen Caimei Printing Co., Ltd.
10   9   8   7   6   5   4   3   2   1

Library of Congress Cataloging-in-Publication Data

Knit Christmas stockings / edited by Gwen W. Steege. — 2nd Edition.
     pages cm
  Includes index.
  ISBN 978-1-61212-252-6 (pbk. : alk. paper)
  ISBN 978-1-61212-253-3 (ebook)
  1. Knitting—Patterns. 2. Christmas stockings. 3. Christmas tree ornaments.
  I. Steege, Gwen, 1940– editor.
TT825.K6233 2013
746.43'2—dc23
                                        2013012522

CONTENTS

Stockings Up!

A hand-knit Christmas stocking is bound to be a treasure for years to come, whether you lovingly knit one as a gift or create a set for your own family. In the pages that follow, we offer a wide variety of styles, so you're sure to find one that's perfect for the spotlight it will claim in your home. Some of our patterns are as traditional as the holidays themselves, while others offer a new twist to classic ideas, with their bright and surprising color combinations. You'll find several felted knitting projects, multicolor patterns, and some interesting textural designs. Some of the stockings are extra large; in contrast, you'll find mini socks, as well as miniature mittens and sweaters just right for hanging on the tree or even packaging small gifts. Everyone seems to want to knit socks these days, and knitting a roomy Christmas stocking is a wonderful way for novice knitters to learn some basic sock-knitting techniques. Plus, no second-sock syndrome: you have to knit only one! So choose a pattern from our collection of talented designers, pick up your needles and yarn, and get set to knit a true Christmas heirloom!

※ ANATOMY OF A SOCK ※

"Real" socks must fit a three-dimensional foot and, for comfort's sake, have few or no seams. Knitted from top to toe, in the round on circular or double-pointed needles, socks are shaped as you knit. Here's a brief rundown of the basic structure to help you envision your sock project as a whole.

Each stocking in this book starts at the top by knitting the cuff and then the leg. When you get to the ankle, you set aside the stitches across the top of the foot (the instep) on a spare needle or stitch holder and, for just this section, knit back and forth on straight needles to create a little rectangle called the heel flap. Next, you pick up stitches along both sides of the heel flap, retrieve the instep stitches, and again begin to knit circularly. To accommodate the wider shape of the foot at the ankle, the diameter of the sock is wider here than at the leg and along the length of the foot, so in order to narrow the stocking again to create the foot, you make a series of decreases at each side of the heel, forming the gusset. When the foot is the desired length, you shape the toe with further reductions. Close off the toe stitches, and your stocking is ready to hang!

Yarns to Yearn For

Today's yarn selection makes knitting more fun than it's ever been before. The stockings in this book were knit with yarns of varied fiber content and weight. We tell you exactly which yarns the pictured stockings were knit with, but we hope that you'll enjoy experimenting with your own color combinations and yarn varieties — wool, cotton, synthetics, and blends, and maybe even luxury fibers. After all, a very special stocking may someday become a family heirloom. The choice is yours, as long as you keep in mind that you must get the gauge indicated by the pattern (see page 10). Also, if you choose one of the felted projects, be sure to use only 100 percent wool or another animal fiber that will shrink effectively (see Yarns for Felting, opposite).

Be sure to buy enough yarn to complete your project. You'll find information about the number of skeins needed for each pattern in this book, along with the weight and yardage of the skeins we used. If you substitute, be sure to compare your yarn's yardage to the pattern requirement. Yardage is usually listed on the label; if not, ask your yarn shop to check the manufacturer's specifications. It's always a good idea to buy an extra skein to avoid running short; most yarn shops accept returns of untouched skeins of yarn as long as you do so within a reasonable length of time. Check your shop's return policy.

SHORT TALK

If you're new to knitting, abbreviations can seem like a foreign language, so in this book we've avoided overusing them as much as possible. Here's what you'll find:

CC	contrasting color	**P2tog**	purl 2 stitches together
K	knit	**psso**	pass slipped stitch over
K2tog	knit 2 stitches together	**ssk**	slip, slip, knit the two slipped stitches together
M1	make 1 stitch		
MC	main color	**yo**	yarn over
P	purl		

YARNS FOR FELTING

Any animal fiber, such as wool, alpaca, and mohair, will felt, as long as it hasn't been pretreated. Washable (superwash) wool, bleached white wool, cotton, rayon, silk, and synthetic fibers don't felt. Many off-white and light colors do not felt well, if at all. It's not unusual to find that different colors of the same yarn felt differently. Some yarns require a longer period of agitation than others, or they may not ever achieve the degree of felting desired. Making swatches is always a good idea, but before jumping into any felted knitting project, it's especially important to knit and felt a swatch with the yarns you've chosen. (For more about felting, see page 125.)

Getting Equipped

Most knitters have strong preferences when it comes to selecting knitting needles, and the wide variety of choices can be confusing until you try them. Coated aluminum needles are durable but sometimes heavy in larger sizes. I find that slippery yarns tend to slide rather easily off metal needles. Plastic or similar materials are lighter, though they can bend or break, and yarn sometimes sticks to them. Depending on the yarn you're working with, bamboo or wood needles may be a good compromise. The yarn moves smoothly along them, even in hot, sticky weather, and they're quiet and comfortable to use.

Most of the patterns in this book are knit on double-pointed or circular needles. Available in several lengths, circular needles have a flexible nylon or plastic center cable. Double-pointed needles come in sets of four or five. If you've always used four for knitting in the round, you'll find knitting with five is easier and less likely to leave telltale lines (known as ladders) between the needles.

The size of knitting needles is indicated by number. It's important to note whether the size is US, UK, or metric — they're all different! The chart on page 8 gives equivalent sizes for all three. You'll note that in the US system 0 is very small, whereas in the UK system 0 is large. This book provides US and metric (but not UK) sizes in all the instructions.

Do Bag It!

Although you can get started on most projects with little more than yarn and needles, a nice, well-supplied knitting bag, like all tool kits, makes life easier. Here are some suggestions for things you might need:

* Straight, circular, and double-pointed needles in assorted sizes

* Crochet hooks in small, medium, and large sizes

* Retractable tape measure and a 6-inch metal ruler with needle gauge

* Needle point protectors, to keep yarn from slipping from needles

* T-pins, to help you block and shape the finished item

* Blunt-tipped tapestry needles, for sewing seams and weaving in ends

* Small, sharp scissors

* Stitch holders, as well as safety pins for holding small numbers of stitches

* Stitch markers, round and split

* Cable needles

* Sticky tags or see-through removable tape, to mark your place in patterns and charts

❄ NEEDLE CONVERSIONS ❄

US	Metric	UK	US	Metric	UK
0	2 mm	14	7	4.5 mm	7
1	2.25 mm	13	8	5 mm	6
	2.5 mm		9	5.5 mm	5
2	2.75 mm	12	10	6 mm	4
	3 mm	11	10½	6.5 mm	3
3	3.25 mm	10		7 mm	2
4	3.5 mm			7.5 mm	1
5	3.75 mm	9	11	8 mm	0
6	4 mm	8	13	9 mm	00
			15	10 mm	000

One Good Turn

You may have heard enthusiastic new sock knitters proudly talk about learning to "turn the heel." Although it may sound somewhat esoteric, there's really no mystery to turning a heel, once you understand the principle. Turning the heel is a key step in shaping the stocking, taking you from the tube that forms the leg, accommodating the larger-diameter section around the ankle, and merging into the slimmed-down area that is the foot.

The heel is turned by working what are known as short rows at the bottom of the heel flap (see Anatomy of a Sock, page 5) while you're still knitting back and forth in rows and before you begin to knit the instep circularly. The number of stitches in the heel flap varies from pattern to pattern, of course, but you are usually instructed to knit about two-thirds of the way across the row, work two stitches together, knit another stitch, and then turn to go back the other way, leaving the remainder of the stitches behind, unworked. The trick is that you must believe this and follow the directions, even if they seem odd to you! If you are working stockinette stitch, you slip the first stitch after you turn, then purl a certain number of stitches, but only as far as the pattern directs. Again, work two stitches together, purl one, and then turn to go back the other way. This is when you see the magic begin! When you come to the place in the row where you turned (just after the two stitches you worked together), you'll see a very noticeable gap between the slipped stitch of the row before and the first unworked stitch. Work the two stitches on either side of the gap together, work the next stitch, and turn. The pattern directions will inform you about the number of stitches to work, but you'll soon get used to the visual clues and be able to confidently anticipate where to decrease. Continue in this way until all the stitches have been worked.

Wrap & Turn

When working short rows as described above, some sock knitters use a "wrap and turn" (W&T) method to eliminate the small hole that may appear when you turn in the middle of a row. *On knit rows,* work up to the turning point, slip the next stitch purlwise onto the right-hand needle with yarn in back. Move the yarn between the needles to the front of the work, return the slipped stitch to the left-hand needle, and turn to work in the other direction. If you're working stockinette stitch, move the yarn between the needles to the front and begin to purl; if you're working garter stitch, leave the yarn at the back and begin to knit: W&T is complete. *On purl rows*, work up to the turning point, then slip the next stitch purlwise onto the right-hand needle with yarn in front. Move the yarn between the needles to the back of the work; return slipped stitch to the left-hand needle, and turn to work in the opposite direction. Move the yarn between the needles to the back and begin to knit: W&T is complete.

Watch Those Swatches

Even though Christmas stockings don't have to fit and you want to get going on your project just as soon as possible, it really does pay to take time to knit a swatch. Gauge matters even when fit doesn't, as the perfect gauge means that your fabric isn't either sleazy because the stitches were too loose, or stiff because the stitches were crammed in too tight. Swatching is how you test the number of stitches per inch you'll be getting with the yarn and needles you're using. Always calculate your gauge over at least 4 inches. That's because counting stitches over just 1 inch can be misleading if your stitches are uneven or the stitch count within that inch comes up with a fraction. Here's an example of how to knit a swatch and figure out gauge:

STEP 1. If the pattern gauge is 16 stitches = 4 inches on size US 7 (4.5 mm) needles, use these needles to cast on about 24 stitches. (You need a few extra stitches so that you don't have to measure the edge stitches, which may be uneven or draw in.)

STEP 2. Following the stitch pattern you'll be using for the main part of your project, knit a swatch about 5 inches long. Block it as you plan to block the finished item.

STEP 3. Lay the swatch on a firm, flat surface, taking care not to stretch it. Uncurl the side edges and lay a flat ruler across the swatch. Count the number of stitches within 4 inches. There should be exactly 16.

STEP 4. *If your swatch contains more* than 16 stitches in 4 inches, use larger needles and knit another swatch, repeating steps 1 through 3. *If your swatch contains fewer* than 16 stitches in 4 inches, use smaller needles and knit another swatch, repeating steps 1 through 3.

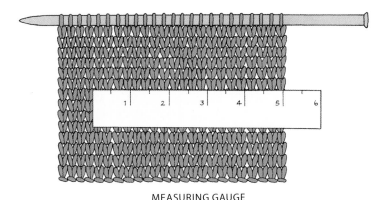

MEASURING GAUGE

NOTE. Always use fresh yarn to check your gauge. Used yarn may have stretched and thus give an inaccurate measurement. Also, if two needle sizes are specified for a pattern and you change your larger-size needles to obtain the correct stitch gauge, adjust the size of the smaller needles to correspond. Finally, even after you have established what needle size and yarn gives the right gauge, check again after you have knitted a few inches into the project to make sure your gauge is holding true.

Casting On

Using a long-tail cast on makes an especially neat, firm but elastic edge. If you tend to cast on tightly, you may want to switch to one needle size larger for this step.

STEP 1. Estimate how long to make the tail by wrapping the yarn around the needle one time for each cast-on stitch you need, then adding a few extra inches. Make a slip knot right here, and slide the knot over a single knitting needle. Hold that needle in your right hand; hold the tail and the working end of the yarn in your left hand as shown. Insert the needle over the front of the tail on your thumb and up through the middle of the loop.

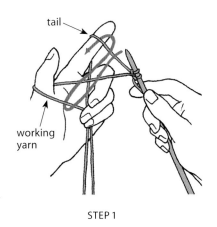

tail

working
yarn

STEP 1

11

STEP 2. Insert the needle over the front of the working yarn on your index finger and draw a loop of it through the loop on your thumb.

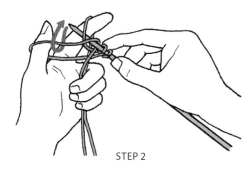

STEP 2

STEP 3. Release the loop on your thumb, place your thumb underneath the tail, and snug the new stitch onto the needle. The stitch should be well formed, but not too tight. As you make additional stitches, try to keep them as consistent as possible.

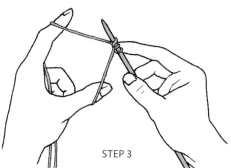

STEP 3

Binding Off

Binding off is sometimes called casting off. The simplest way to bind off is to work two stitches, then draw the first one over the second. Don't pull too tightly, or your edge will be puckered and inelastic. Continue to work a stitch, then carry the stitch already on the needle over the newly made one. When you reach the last stitch, pull the working end through the stitch.

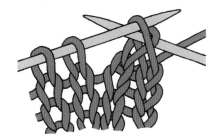

BINDING OFF

Loose-Method Bind Off

If you tend to bind off tightly, you may want to switch to one needle size larger. Or, try this:

STEP 1. Work two stitches. Insert your needle in the first stitch, use the left-hand needle to draw it over the second stitch, but instead of completing the bind off and dropping the first stitch, leave it on the left needle.

LOOSE-METHOD
BIND OFF, STEP 1

STEP 2. As you work the next stitch, allow the first stitch to drop off the needle.

Continue in this way until all stitches are bound off.

LOOSE-METHOD
BIND OFF, STEP 2

Three-Needle Bind Off

This is a useful technique if you want to bind off and join two pieces in an invisible seam at the same time. Place half the stitches on one needle and half on a second needle. Holding the needles in your left hand, bring the two pieces, or two halves, together with the right sides facing. The tips should be pointing in the same direction, with the yarn attached to one of the halves at the beginning of the needle.

STEP 1. Insert a third needle through the first stitches on the front and back needles, and knit them together.

STEP 2. Make a second stitch in the same way, and then pass the first stitch over the second one. Repeat until you've bound off all stitches.

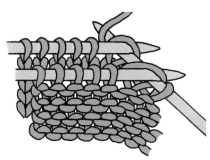

THREE-NEEDLE BIND OFF

NOTE: Instead of executing this technique with right sides together, which creates an invisible seam on the right side of the fabric, you can do it with wrong sides together, creating an interesting raised design element on the fabric.

On the Decrease

As with increasing, decreasing can become an interesting design element in your project, and pattern directions usually specify which method to use. The three techniques shown here are the most common. Because the first two (ssk and psso) result in a finished stitch that slants to the left, they are often used at the right-hand side of an item; the last method (K2tog) results in a right-slanting stitch and so is used on the left-hand edge.

ssk

The first method is called "ssk" (slip, slip, knit the two slipped stitches together). Slip two stitches, one at a time, from your left-hand needle to your right, as if to knit (knitwise). Then slide the left-hand needle from left to right through the front loops of the slipped stitches, and knit the two stitches together

SSK

from this position. This technique makes a finished stitch that slants to the left on the finished side and is often used at the beginning of a row.

psso

To "psso" (pass slipped stitch over knit stitch), slip one stitch from the left- to the right-hand needle, inserting the needle as if to knit the stitch, but without knitting it. Knit the next stitch, then draw the slipped stitch over the just-knitted stitch. The finished stitch will slant to the left on the finished side.

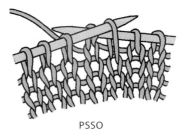

PSSO

K2tog

For a finished stitch that slants to the right on the finished side, simply knit two stitches together by inserting the needle into both loops, just as you would to knit. K2tog (knit 2 together) is generally used at the end of a row.

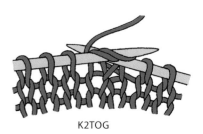

K2TOG

On the Increase

Increases allow you to shape your knitting as you work. Sometimes you'll want these increases to be invisible, but in other cases the increase stitches are not only noticeable but important design elements. It's helpful to learn a variety of techniques so that you can pick and choose whatever is appropriate for your needs. The illustrations that follow show three increase methods: bar increase, make 1 with a right slant, and make 1 with a left slant.

Bar Increase

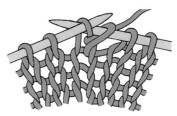

The bar increase is a tight increase that leaves no hole but shows as a short, horizontal bar on the right side of the fabric. Make it by knitting into the front of the loop in the usual way, but do not remove

BAR INCREASE

the stitch from the needle. Instead, knit into the back of the same stitch, and slip both new stitches onto the right-hand needle. This is often called a knit-front-back (kfb) increase.

For a bar increase of two stitches, work into the front loop, the back loop, and the front loop again before taking the three new stitches off the needle.

Make 1, right slant

STEP 1. Look for the horizontal bar between the first stitch on your left-hand needle and the last stitch on your right-hand needle. With the tip of your left needle, pick up this bar from back to front.

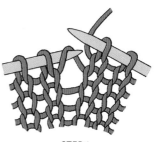

STEP 1

STEP 2. Knit into the bar from the front, which twists the new stitch and gives it a slant to the right. Even though it may seem a bit difficult to get your needle into the bar from front to back, it's important to do so in order to avoid creating a small hole in the fabric.

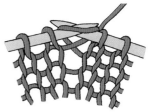

STEP 2

Make 1, left slant

STEP 1. Again using the tip of your left-hand needle, pick up the horizontal bar between the first stitch on your left-hand needle and the last stitch on your right-hand needle, this time from front to back.

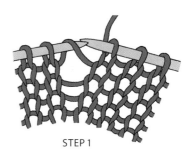

STEP 1

STEP 2. Now, knit into the back of the bar, which twists the new stitch to the left.

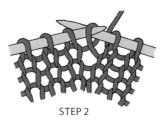

STEP 2

NOTE: To make 1 at the end of a round, pick up the horizontal strand between the first and the last stitch of the round.

Getting Around

Most of the knitting in this book is done on either circular or double-pointed needles, using a technique known as working in the round. Since you shape the item as you knit, there's usually little or no assembly to worry about once the knitting is complete. To make stockinette stitch when you knit in the round, you always knit on the right side, continuing around the circular or double-pointed needles without ever turning your work. (On straight needles, stockinette is created by knitting on one side, turning, and purling on the return.)

TO KNIT WITH DOUBLE-POINTED NEE-DLES, cast on the correct number of stitches for your project, and divide the stitches evenly among three (or four, if you're using a five-needle set) of the needles (or as the pattern directs). Lay the work on a flat surface, forming the three needles into

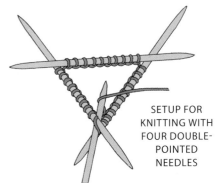

SETUP FOR KNITTING WITH FOUR DOUBLE-POINTED NEEDLES

a triangle (or forming four needles into a square). Arrange the cast-on stitches so they are flat and their bases all face toward the center of the triangle. Look carefully along the needles, and especially at the corners, to make sure that the stitches don't take an extra twist around the needle.

The next step is the trickiest: Carefully lift the needles, keeping the stitches aligned, and use the working yarn that formed the last cast-on stitch to knit the first stitch on the left-hand needle. Snug the yarn firmly before knitting the second stitch. (Do not tie to join.) Knit across until the left-hand needle is empty. Use the empty needle to knit the stitches on the next needle. Continue knitting until the first round is complete. Place a split-stitch marker or a safety pin on the fabric between the first and last stitches to indicate the beginning of each new round, or use the cast-on tail to keep track.

※ **TRADING PLACES** ※

Knitting designer Betsy Lee McCarthy (see her pattern on page 32) offers this tip for making a smooth, secure join when getting started to knit in the round: Distribute the stitches among the needles as indicated in the pattern, then check to make sure they are not twisted. Hold the needle with the first cast-on stitch in your left hand, and the needle with the working yarn and the last cast-on stitch in your right hand. Place the skein so it will be outside the circle once the yarn is joined. With the tip of the right-hand needle, slip the first stitch on the left-hand needle to the right-hand needle. With the left-hand needle, lift the last cast-on stitch on the right-hand needle up and over the first stitch and onto the left-hand needle. It is now the new first stitch on the left-hand needle. In other words, make the first and last stitches of the cast on trade places. Pull both ends of the yarn to snug up. You may want to place a marker between the two stitches to indicate the beginning of the round.

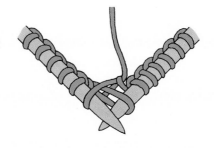

TO KNIT WITH CIRCULAR NEEDLES, cast on the correct number of stitches as usual, then lay the work on a flat surface. Arrange the stitches so that they face the center of the circle and carefully knit the first couple of stitches on the left-hand needle, taking care not to twist any stitches around the needles. Snug the yarn tightly between the last cast-on stitch and the first stitch in the first round. (Do not tie to join.) Place a marker between these two stitches to help you keep track of rounds.

Tips for Success with Circles

Knitting in the round can be relaxing and fun if you develop just a few good habits. Here are some tips to make it easier:

❁ To avoid those loose stitches that often develop where you change needles (often called ladders), snug the yarn firmly after you knit the first stitch on the new needle.

❁ Arrange your needles so the ends of the two you are working with lie on top of the nonworking needle(s).

❁ Use a stitch marker, safety pin, or colored yarn to mark the first stitch of the round.

❁ Never reverse directions!

Joining New Yarn

When you run out of yarn and need to start a new end, do so toward the edge of the stocking, where the join is less likely to be noticed. To make the join, lay the new end along the back of the work, and carry it forward for six or seven stitches by weaving the working yarn over and under it as you knit, in much the same way that you handle a second color yarn in multicolor knitting (see The Joy of Color, right). Once it is snugly woven in in this manner you can simply pick it up and begin knitting with it. Weave in the tail of the old

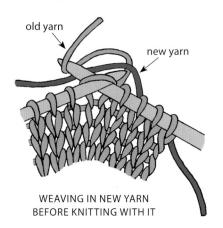

old yarn

new yarn

WEAVING IN NEW YARN
BEFORE KNITTING WITH IT

yarn when your work is complete. If you follow this procedure faithfully throughout a project, you will have few ends to darn in — and you'll thank yourself heartily for that!

The Joy of Color

You can create an infinite number of fascinating designs by knitting with two or more colors in a single row or round. The multicolor knitting in this book is called stranded knitting, in which two (or more) colors interchange regularly all the way across the row. We illustrate the sequence of colors in charts that are color-matched to the photos of the finished projects. Begin charts at the bottom right. (The words *start here* and an arrow will help you find your place.)

When you change colors within a row, always take the color you want to emphasize from below the other. On the front, the color handled this way will dominate the pattern and create a more uniform design. Be sure to be consistent and take the same yarn over and the other under throughout the project.

When you knit with more than one color, carry the other color or colors along on the wrong side. Keep the carried yarn loose and don't carry it for more than three stitches. For wider runs in the pattern, catch the carried yarn by wrapping the working yarn around it from underneath every three or four stitches.

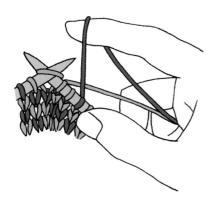

LIFTING DARK COLOR
OVER LIGHT ONE

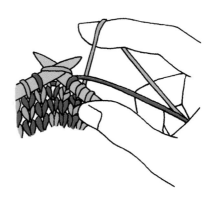

BRINGING LIGHT YARN
FROM UNDERNEATH

Hiding Color Jogs in Stripes

Designers Deb and Lynda Gemmell (see their pattern on page 70) offer this tip for making a smooth transition from one color to the next: Sew the tails with a yarn needle from the beginnings of the stripes up and to the left. Sew the tails from the ends of the stripes down and to the right. This trick helps disguise the "jog" where a new color starts.

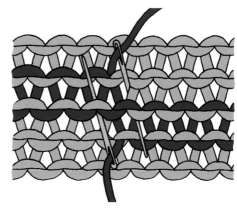

HIDING A COLOR JOG

EASY PICKUP

Beginning knitters often panic when they drop a stitch. It's empowering to discover how easy it is to pick up dropped or half-made stitches. Working on the right side of stockinette stitch, find the last loop that's still knitted and insert a crochet hook from front to back. Pull the loop just above the bar between the adjacent stitches, catch the bar with your hook, and draw it through the loop. If you have to pick up a number of stitches, take care to pick up the bars in the correct order.

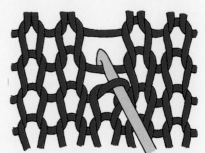

PICKING UP A DROPPED
STITCH KNITWISE

Stocking Blocking

You may be anxious to see your beautiful new creation hung by the chimney with care, but do take the time to weave in any loose ends you missed on the wrong side of the fabric, then block it properly. You'll be surprised at how unevenness disappears when you block your knitting.

You can steam-block all-wool fabrics by holding a steam iron just above the surface so the steam penetrates the fabric, or cover the surface with a wet pressing cloth and lightly touch the iron to it. Either way, avoid pressing hard or moving the iron back and forth. Never iron or block a ribbed hem; it will lose its elasticity.

For wool blends, mohair, angora, alpaca, or cashmere, just dampen the knitted piece by spraying it lightly with water, then pin it to a flat surface where you can safely leave it to air-dry. Be sure to pin it so that corners and the stitches line up straight.

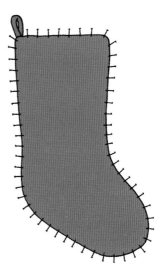

BLOCKING BY PINNING
SOCK OUT TO SIZE

Winter Wonderland

DESIGNED BY BARBARA TELFORD

Snowflakes, snowballs, and snowmen dance around this winter wonderland of a stocking, and two more snowmen dangle from the ends of the drawstring. Their pompom hats and jaunty red scarves give them flair worthy of any blizzard.

FINISHED MEASUREMENTS

❄ 5½" wide x 19" long

YARN

Cascade 220, 100% Peruvian Highland wool, worsted weight, 3½ oz (100 g)/220 yd (200 m) skeins

❄ **MC**   Blue Velvet (7818), 1 skein

❄ **CC A**   Granny Smith (8914), 1 skein

❄ **CC B**   Shire (2445), 1 skein

❄ **CC C**   Natural (8010), 1 skein

❄ **CC D**   Peacock (2433), 1 skein

❄ **CC E**   Christmas Red (8895), 4 yds

ABBREVIATIONS

CC	contrasting color
K	knit
K2tog	knit 2 stitches together
MC	main color
P	purl
P2tog	purl 2 stitches together
psso	pass slipped stitch over
ssk	slip, slip, knit the 2 slipped stitches together
yo	yarn over

NEEDLES

❄ One set of US 6 (4 mm) double-pointed needles *or size you need to obtain correct gauge*

❄ One set of double-pointed needles two sizes smaller than gauge needle

GAUGE

❄ 22 stitches = 4" on US 6 (4 mm) needles in stockinette stitch

OTHER SUPPLIES

❄ Graph paper and pencil

❄ Stitch holder or spare needle

❄ Yarn needle

❄ 2 yds each of black and orange worsted-weight yarn (for CC F and CC G, respectively), 4/E (3.5 mm) or 6/G (4 mm) crochet hook

❄ Small amount of polyester fiberfill stuffing for the snowmen dangles

❄ Liquid seam sealant such as Fray Check

Knitting the Cuff

SETUP: With smaller double-pointed needles and MC, cast on 60 stitches. Distribute stitches evenly among three needles. Join the knitting into a round, being careful not to twist the stitches (see Getting Around, page 16).

ROUND 1: *K1, P1; repeat from * to the end of the round.

NEXT ROUNDS: Continue working in K1, P1 ribbing until cuff measures 1".

NEXT ROUND: Change to larger needles and knit to the end of the round.

Making the Eyelets

ROUND 1: K3, slip 1, K1, psso, *K4, slip 1, K1, psso; repeat from * to the last stitch, K1. *You now have* 50 stitches.

ROUND 2: K3, yo, *K5, yo; repeat from * to the last 2 stitches, K2.

ROUND 3: Knit to the end of the round. (Knit the yo stitches from the previous round as normal stitches). *You now have* 60 stitches again.

Knitting the Leg

ROUNDS 1–4: Using CC A and CC B and working even in stockinette stitch, follow the Checkerboard 1 chart on page 30. Start where indicated on line 1 at the bottom and work from right to left, repeating the pattern 15 times around the stocking. (For information about knitting with several colors, see The Joy of Color on page 19.)

ROUNDS 5–13: Using MC and CC A, work a name or message in these 9 rounds. Create your own chart on graph paper, using the Alphabet chart on page 69 for guidance. If possible, allow 1 stitch between letters and 3 stitches between words. You may also knit these rows with MC and add the letters later in Duplicate Stitch (see page 111).

ROUNDS 14–17: Using CC A and CC B, repeat rounds 1–4 of Checkerboard 1 chart.

ROUNDS 18–23: Using MC and CC C, follow the Snowball chart on page 30, starting with line 1 at the bottom and working from right to left, repeating the pattern six times around the stocking. To make the snowball bobbles, see Making Bobbles on page 29.

ROUNDS 24–36: Using MC and CC C, follow the Snowflake chart on page 31. Start where indicated on line 1 at the bottom and work from right to left, repeating the pattern six times around the stocking.

ROUNDS 37–42: Using MC and CC C, repeat rounds 18–23 of the Snowball chart.

ROUNDS 43–46: Using CC A and CC C, repeat rounds 1–4 of the Checkerboard 2 chart.

ROUNDS 47–66: Using CC C, CC D, CC E, and CC F, follow the Snowman chart on page 31. Start where indicated on line 1 at the bottom and work from right to left, repeating pattern six times around the stocking. To make each snowman's nose and the pompom on his hat, see Making Bobbles on page 29. Cut short pieces of CC F yarn for the snowmen's eyes and buttons rather than carrying the yarn behind the work.

Making the Heel Flap

NOTE: *In this section and the next, work back and forth on two needles.*

ROW 1 (RIGHT SIDE): Using CC D, K30. Slide the remaining stitches to a stitch holder or spare needle. Turn.

ROW 2 (WRONG SIDE): Using CC A and CC B, P1 with CC A, *P2 with CC B, P2 with CC A; repeat from * to the last stitch, P1 with CC B.

ROW 3: K1 with CC A, *K2 with CC B, K2 with CC A; repeat from * to the last stitch, K1 with CC B.

ROW 4: P1 with CC B, *P2 with CC A, P2 with CC B; repeat from * to the last stitch, P1 with CC A.

ROW 5: K1 with CC A, *K2 with CC B, K2 with CC A; repeat from * to the last stitch, K1 with CC B.

ROWS 6–17: Repeat rows 2–5 three more times.

Turning the Heel

ROW 1: Using CC D, P20, P2tog, P1, turn. *(7 stitches remain unworked on needle.)*

ROW 2: Slip 1, K11, ssk, K1, turn. *(7 stitches remain unworked on needle.)*

ROW 3: Slip 1, P11, P2tog, P1, turn. *(6 stitches remain unworked on needle.)*

NEXT ROWS: Repeat rows 2 and 3 until 14 stitches remain on the needle, ending with a knit row.

Knitting the Gusset and Foot

NOTE: *Begin again to knit in the round. For information on how to pick up stitches along the heel, see Picking Up Stitches, page 92.*

SETUP:

- ❄ With the needle holding the 14 heel stitches and using CC D, pick up and knit 12 stitches from the side of the heel flap. This will now be called Needle 3.
- ❄ With a new needle, K30 from the stitch holder. This will now be called Needle 1.
- ❄ With a new needle, pick up and knit 12 stitches from the other side of the heel flap. This will now be called Needle 2. K7 from Needle 3 onto Needle 2.

You now have 68 stitches, distributed as follows:

> **Needle 1:** 30 stitches
>
> **Needle 2:** 19 stitches
>
> **Needle 3:** 19 stitches

ROUND 1: Using CC A and CC C, knit to end of round, following Checkerboard 2 chart on page 30. Begin where indicated on line 1 and repeat the pattern 17 times around the stocking. Since you are knitting in the round again, work all lines of the chart from right to left. In rounds 2–4, adjust to account for decreases at sides so that you maintain the checkerboard pattern.

ROUND 2:

> **Needle 1:** K30.
>
> **Needle 2:** K1, K2tog, knit to the end of the needle.
>
> **Needle 3:** Knit to the last 3 stitches, ssk, K1.

You now have 66 stitches, distributed as follows:

> **Needle 1:** 30 stitches
>
> **Needle 2:** 18 stitches
>
> **Needle 3:** 18 stitches

ROUND 3: Knit to the end of the round.

ROUND 4: Decrease as in round 2. *You now have* 64 stitches.

ROUND 5: With MC and CC C, begin working the Snowball chart, on page 30. Knit to the end of the round.

ROUND 6: Decrease as in round 2. *You now have* 62 stitches as in round 4.

ROUND 7: Knit to the end of the round.

ROUND 8:

Needle 1: K5, make Snowball bobble (see Making Bobbles, page 29) in the next stitch, K9, make Snowball in the next stitch, K9, make Snowball in the next stitch, K4.

Needle 2: K1, K2tog, K3, make Snowball in the next stitch, K9.

Needle 3: Make Snowball in the first stitch, K9, make Snowball in the next stitch, K2, ssk, K1.

You now have 60 stitches (30/15/15).

ROUNDS 9 AND 10: Work the last 2 rounds of the Snowball chart.

ROUNDS 11–23: With MC and CC C, work the Snowflake chart.

ROUNDS 24–29: With MC and CC C, work the Snowball chart.

ROUNDS 30–33: With CC A and CC B, work the Checkerboard 1 chart .

Shaping the Toe

ROUNDS 1 AND 2: Using MC, knit to the end of each round.

ROUND 3:

Needle 1: K1, K2tog, knit to the last 3 stitches, ssk, K1.

Needle 2: K1, K2tog, knit to the end of the needle.

Needle 3: Knit to the last 3 stitches, ssk, K1.

You now have 56 stitches (28/14/14).

NEXT ROUNDS: Repeat round 3 until a total of 12 stitches remains (6/3/3).

Slide the stitches from Needle 3 onto Needle 2, and use Kitchener stitch to graft these stitches together with the stitches on Needle 1. (See Kitchener Stitch, page 93.)

Making the Snowman Dangles (make 2)

NOTE: *Refer to Snowman Dangle chart on page 31 as you work rows 1–22 below. Cut short pieces of CC F yarn for the snowmen's eyes and buttons rather than carrying the yarn behind the work.*

ROW 1: With CC C and larger needles, cast on 3 stitches.

ROWS 2 AND 4: Purl to the end of each row.

ROW 3: Increase 2 in each stitch by knitting into the front, then into the back, then into the front again before slipping the stitch from the needle. *You now have 9 stitches.*

ROW 5: Increase 1 in each of the first 4 stitches by knitting into the front and then into the back before slipping from the needle; K1, increase 1 in each of the last 4 stitches as before. *You now have 17 stitches.*

ROWS 6–11: Work even in stockinette stitch, consulting the Snowman Dangle chart on page 31 for the placement of the snowman's buttons.

ROW 12: P2tog four times, P1, P2tog four times. *You now have 9 stitches.*

ROW 13: (K1, knit into front and back of next stitch) four times, K1. *You now have 13 stitches.*

ROWS 14–18: Work even in stockinette stitch, consulting the Snowman Dangle chart on page 31 for the placement of the snowman's eyes and nose in rows 15 and 16. To make the bobble for the snowman's nose, see Making Bobbles, right.

ROW 19: K2tog three times, K1, K2tog three times. *You now have 7 stitches.*

ROWS 20 AND 22: Purl to the end of each row.

ROW 21: K2tog, slip 1, K2tog, psso, K2tog. *You now have 3 stitches.*

Cut yarn, leaving a tail long enough to sew a seam, and pull it through the remaining stitches.

MAKING BOBBLES

This stocking features bobbles knitted into the pattern bands and into the snowman dangles. Bobbles are made by knitting several stitches into a single stitch, working on these expanded stitches for one or more rows, and reducing them back to a single stitch.

SNOWBALL (S). To make the snowball bobble, with CC C knit 4 stitches into the marked stitch (knit into the front, back, front, and back of the same stitch before dropping it off the needle). Turn, P4. Turn, K4. Turn, P4. Turn, K4tog through the back of the stitches. With the left-hand needle, pick up the stitch that the bobble was made in, knit it with MC, and pass the bobble stitch over it.

POMPOM (P). To make the pompom in the snowman's hat, with CC C knit 2 stitches into the marked stitch (knit into the front and back of the same stitch before dropping it off the needle). Turn, P2. Turn, K2tog through the back of the stitches. With the left-hand needle, pick up the stitch that the bobble was made in, knit it with CC D, and pass the bobble stitch over it.

SNOWMAN'S NOSE (N). To make the snowman's nose, with CC G, K1, slip the left needle into the front of this stitch and knit. Repeat this until you have a chain of 7 stitches. Pick up the stitch at the bottom of the carrot nose, knit it with CC C, and pass the bobble stitch over it.

Making the I-Cord

With CC D and larger needles, cast on 3 stitches.

Make an 18" I-cord (see We've Got Hang-Ups, page 77).

Finishing

Weave in all loose ends with yarn needle on the wrong side.

Fold each snowman in half lengthwise, right sides together. Sew the seam from top to bottom, leaving a small hole for stuffing at the bottom. Stuff the snowman dangles and complete sewing the seam.

(continued on next page)

Finishing (CONTINUED)

With CC E and the crochet hook, make an 18-chain scarf for each snowman dangle and for each snowman on the stocking. Tug the ends of the chains tight and secure them with a drop of liquid seam sealant. Pull each scarf through the stitches on each side of the snowman's neck and tie them to look like scarves.

Thread the I-cord through the eyelets at the top of the stocking. Sew the snowman dangles to the ends of the I-cord.

KEY

■	MC	Blue Velvet
■	CC A	Granny Smith
■	CC B	Shire
□	CC C	Natural
■	CC D	Peacock
■	CC E	Christmas Red
■	CC F	black
▥	CC G	orange
S	Snowman Bobble	
P	Popcorn	
N	Snowman's Nose	

CHECKERBOARD 1

← Start here

CHECKERBOARD 2

← Start here

SNOWBALL

← Start here

Note: *It is customary in knitting books for charts to be followed from bottom to top, and, when knitting circularly, from right to left. Although this results in some charts apparently being presented upside down, the designs will be right side up when the stocking is completed.*

SNOWMAN

SNOWFLAKE

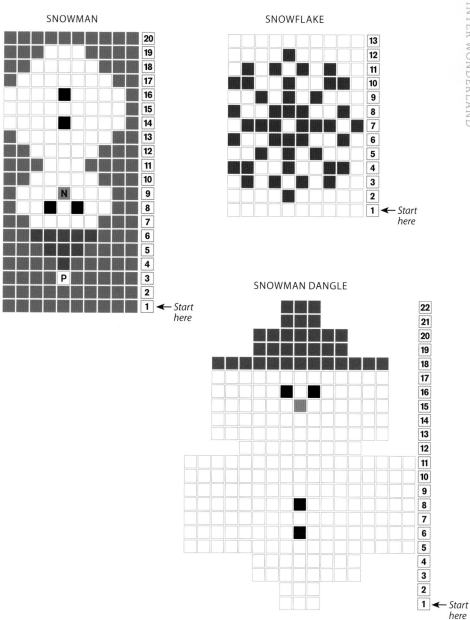

SNOWMAN DANGLE

Rustic Lodge

Designed by Betsy Lee McCarthy

The roll-top cuff is a simple, innovative beginning for a colorful sock that will look great by any fireplace. Besides being quick to knit, the bulky wool-tweed yarn adds a bit of rustic charm. A great project for beginners, the stocking comes in two sizes, both knit firmly for added durability. One large and one small stocking can be made from three skeins of the main color of the yarn listed and two skeins in a contrasting color, if you reverse the colors used for the parts of the stockings.

FINISHED MEASUREMENTS

※ Small, 5" wide x 12" long

※ Large, 7½" wide x 17½" long

YARN

Berroco Blackstone Tweed Chunky, 65% wool/25% superkid mohair/10% angora rabbit hair, 1.75 oz (50 g)/60 yd (55 m) skeins

Small
MC	Concord (6645), 1 skein
CC	Cranberry Bog (6614), 1 skein

Large
MC	Cranberry Bog (6614), 2 skeins
CC	Concord (6645), 1 skein

NEEDLES

※ One set of five US 9 (5.5 mm) double-pointed needles *or size you need to obtain correct gauge*

GAUGE

※ 15½ stitches = 4" on US 9 (5.5 mm) double-pointed needles in stockinette stitch

OTHER SUPPLIES

※ Large crochet hook (size G/6 [4 mm] or H/8 [5 mm]), yarn needle

ABBREVIATIONS

CC	contrasting color	P2tog	purl 2 stitches together
K	knit	rnd(s)	round(s)
K2tog	knit 2 stitches together	ssk	slip, slip, knit the 2 slipped stitches together
MC	main color	st(s)	stitch(es)
P	purl		

Knitting the Top and Leg

	SMALL	LARGE
SETUP: Using CC, cast on	36 sts	52 sts
Distribute stitches evenly among four needles and join into a round, being careful not to twist the stitches. (See Trading Places on page 17.) On each needle, *you now have*	9 sts	13 sts
Working circularly, purl to end of each round until the unrolled cuff measures	1¾"	2"
Cut CC. Using MC, knit to the end of each round until the leg measured from where MC began is	6"	10"
In the last round, stop after completing Needle 3.		

Making the Heel Flap

	SMALL	LARGE
On Needle 4, using CC,	K9	K13
Knit all stitches from Needle 1 onto Needle 4 to make the heel flap. This needle, which now becomes Needle 1, has	18 sts	26 sts

NOTE: *To make the heel, you will work flat (back and forth in rows) on Needle 1 stitches, turning after each row. The instep stitches wait on Needles 2 and 3.*

ROW 1 (WRONG SIDE): Slip 1, purl to the end of the row, turn.

ROW 2 (RIGHT SIDE): Slip 1, knit to the end of the row, turn.

	SMALL	LARGE
Repeat rows 1 and 2 until the heel flap measures approximately	2¾"	3¾"

Stop after completing a knit row.

Turning the Heel

NOTE: *You begin turning the heel on the wrong side.*

	SMALL	LARGE
ROW 1: ___, P2tog, P1.	P11	P15
Turn, leaving the following number of stitches unworked:	4 sts	8 sts

ROW 2: Slip 1, K5, ssk, K1.

	SMALL	LARGE
Turn, leaving the following number of stitches unworked:	4 sts	8 sts

ROW 3: Slip 1, P6, P2tog, P1.

ROW 4: Slip 1, K7, ssk, K1, turn.

ROW 5: Slip 1, P8, P2tog, P1, turn.

ROW 6: Slip 1, K9, ssk, K1, turn.

For small size only:

	SMALL	LARGE
Heel is complete. *You now have* Go to Knitting the Gusset (below).	12 sts	—

For large size only:

ROW 7: Slip 1, P10, P2tog, P1, turn.

ROW 8: Slip 1, K11, ssk, K1, turn.

ROW 9: Slip 1, P12, P2tog, P1, turn.

ROW 10: Slip 1, K13, ssk, K1, turn.

	SMALL	LARGE
Heel is complete. *You now have*	—	16 sts

Knitting the Gusset

NOTE: *For information on how to pick up stitches along the heel, see Picking Up Stitches, page 92.*

	SMALL	LARGE
Using MC and an empty needle, pick up and knit along right edge of heel flap	7 sts	9 sts
Continuing with MC, knit the instep stitches on Needles 2 and 3	9 sts	13 sts
With another empty needle, pick up and knit along the left-hand edge of the heel flap	7 sts	9 sts
On the same needle, knit from the heel stitches (half of those remaining after turning the heel)	6 sts	8 sts

Slip the remaining heel stitches to Needle 1.

	SMALL	LARGE
At this point, begin to knit circularly again.		
❄ On Needles 1 and 4, *you now have*	13 sts	17 sts
❄ On Needles 2 and 3, *you now have*	9 sts	13 sts

ROUND 1:

> **Needle 1:** Knit to the last 3 stitches, K2tog, K1.
>
> **Needle 2:** Knit to the end of the needle.
>
> **Needle 3:** Knit to the end of the needle.
>
> **Needle 4:** K1, ssk, knit to the end of the needle.

ROUND 2: Knit to the end of the round.

ROUNDS 3–8: Repeat rounds 1 and 2, decreasing 2 stitches in each odd-numbered round, until each of the four needles has	9 sts	13 sts

Knitting the Foot

Using MC, knit even for	10 rnds	14 rnds
Using CC, knit even for	5 rnds	6 rnds
For large size only:		
K8, K2tog, K15, K2tog, K15, K2tog, K8.		
You now have	36 sts	49 sts

Shaping the Toe

NOTE: *The large size has 2 extra rounds at the beginning of the toe.*

For large size only:		
NEXT ROUND: *K5, K2tog; repeat from * to the end of the round. *You now have*	—	42 sts
NEXT ROUND: Knit to the end of the round.		

Both sizes:	SMALL	LARGE
ROUND 1: *K4, K2tog; repeat from * to the end of the round.		
You now have	30 sts	35 sts
ROUNDS 2, 4, 6, AND 8: Knit to the end of the round.		
ROUND 3: *K3, K2tog; repeat from * to the end of the round.		
You now have	24 sts	28 sts
ROUND 5: *K2, K2tog; repeat from * to the end of the round.		
ROUND 7: *K1, K2tog; repeat from * to the end of the round.		
ROUND 9: *K2tog; repeat from * to the end of the round.		
You now have	6 sts	7 sts

Cut yarn, leaving a 10" tail. Thread the tail through the yarn needle, draw it through the remaining stitches, and pull firmly to secure. Weave in the end on the wrong side of work.

Making the Loop

Cut two strands of MC and two strands of CC, each 30". Hang them over a hook, or get someone to hold them for you. With four strands in each hand, twist each group clockwise until the groups are equally tight and kinked. Hold the two groups together and twist counterclockwise. The two groups will automatically twist together into an attractive and sturdy cord. With the large crochet hook, pull one end of cord through stocking under the roll top and tie or fasten down as desired. Knot the ends and trim off the excess.

Finishing

With a yarn needle, weave in any loose ends. Block the stocking with steam (see Stocking Blocking, page 21). If you want two rolls at the stocking top, roll the top CC band down far enough so that the MC roll appears.

Reindeer & Bells

DESIGNED BY GWEN STEEGE

Add a touch of the Gaelic to your holiday decorations with this Aran-influenced design. Both cables are taken from Barbara Walker's A Second Treasury of Knitting Patterns. *Walker's Staghorn Cable reminds me of a reindeer's antlers, and the Coin Cable, of bells or Christmas tree balls. The creamy white yarn is a traditional choice for Aran knitting, but this stocking would also look great in bright, holiday colors. The choice is yours.*

FINISHED MEASUREMENTS

※ 5" wide x 17" long

YARN

Wool Pak Yarns NZ 10 ply, 100% wool, worsted weight, 8 oz (250 g)/430 yd (393 m), Natural, 1 skein

ABBREVIATIONS

K	knit
K2tog	knit 2 stitches together
P	purl
P2tog	purl 2 stitches together
ssk	slip, slip, knit the 2 slipped stitches together

NEEDLES

※ Two US 7 (4.5 mm) circular needles, 16" long, *or size you need to obtain correct gauge*

GAUGE

※ 18 stitches = 4" on US 7 (4.5 mm) needles in stockinette stitch

OTHER SUPPLIES

※ Stitch markers, cable or double-pointed needle, stitch holder, yarn needle

Knitting the Hemmed Cuff

SETUP: Cast on 64 stitches. Taking care not to twist the stitches, join to work circularly (see Getting Around, page 16).

ROUNDS 1–8: Purl to the end of the round (reverse stockinette stitch).

THE HEM: Use the second circular needle to pick up one loop of each cast-on stitch. Fold the knitting so that the purl side (with "bumps") faces out and the two circular needles are side by side, with about half the stitches on the needles and the working yarn at the needle tips. (You may find it easier to execute this step in stages, picking up only 15 or 20 stitches from the cast on at a time.) Knit together 1 stitch from each needle — 1 from the cast on and 1 from the last round purled.

With the hem complete, *you now have* 64 stitches on one circular needle again. Use a stitch marker to mark the beginning of the rounds.

Knitting the Leg

Work the Reindeer and Bells chart on page 43, beginning as indicated on round 1, line 1 at the lower right and following the chart from right to left. The pattern repeats twice around. Repeat the 6 rounds 9 more times, then work rounds 1 and 2 once more.

Making the Heel Flap

For Mock Cable instructions, see page 43. You may wish to follow the Heel Flap chart (page 43) for rows 1–14 below.

SETUP: Slip 1, (K2, P1) twice, (K1, slip 1) nine times, P1, (K2, P1) twice. Put the remaining 32 stitches (instep stitches) on a holder. Turn.

ROW 1 (WRONG SIDE): Slip 1, purl to the end of the row.

ROW 2 (RIGHT SIDE): Slip 1, (K2, P1) twice, (K1, slip 1) nine times, P1, (K2, P1) twice.

ROW 3: Slip 1, purl to the end of the row.

ROW 4: Slip 1, (Mock Cable, P1) twice, (K1, slip 1) nine times, P1, (Mock Cable, P1) twice.

ROWS 5–14: Repeat rows 3 and 4.

Turning the Heel

ROW 1: Slip 1, K19, ssk, K1, turn. (*9 stitches remain unworked.*)

ROW 2: Slip 1, P9, P2tog, P1, turn. (*9 stitches remain unworked.*)

ROW 3: Slip 1, K10, K2tog, K1, turn. (*7 stitches remain unworked.*)

ROW 4: Slip 1, P11, P2tog, P1, turn. (*7 stitches remain unworked.*)

NEXT ROWS: Continue to work the pattern as established, knitting or purling together the 2 stitches on each side of the gap formed in the previous row until you have worked all the stitches in the row. (The next-to-last row ends ssk; the last row ends P2tog.)

You now have 20 stitches.

Knitting the Gusset and Foot

SETUP: To begin working in the round again, K20 (the heel flap stitches); pick up 13 stitches along the left-hand side of the heel flap, place a marker, work across the instep stitches waiting on the holder continuing the Reindeer and Bells pattern as established; pick up 13 stitches along the right-hand side of the heel flap; place a marker.

You now have 78 stitches: 32 instep stitches and 46 heel/sole stitches.

ROUND 1: K1, K2tog, knit to 3 stitches before the marker, ssk, K1, work pattern across instep stitches to the marker.

ROUND 2: Work the established pattern with no decreases.

NEXT ROUNDS: Repeat rounds 1 and 2 six more times until you have 32 heel/sole stitches.

You now have 64 stitches in all.

NEXT ROUNDS: Continue in established pattern until stocking is 2" less than the desired length.

Shaping the Toe

ROUND 1: (Mock Cable, P1) around, ending Mock Cable, P2tog.

You now have 63 stitches.

ROUND 2: Knit to the end of the round.

ROUND 3: Repeat round 1.

ROUND 4: *K19, K2tog; repeat to the end of the round.

You now have 60 stitches.

ROUND 5: Knit to the end of the round.

ROUND 6: *K4, K2tog; repeat to the end of the round.

You now have 50 stitches.

ROUNDS 7, 9, 11, AND 13: Knit to the end of the round.

ROUND 8: *K3, K2tog; repeat to the end of the round.

You now have 40 stitches.

ROUND 10: *K2, K2tog; repeat to the end of the round.

You now have 30 stitches.

ROUND 12: *K1, K2tog; repeat to the end of the round.

You now have 20 stitches.

ROUND 14: K2tog to the end of the round.

You now have 10 stitches.

Cut yarn, leaving a 10" tail. Thread the tail onto a yarn needle and draw it through the remaining stitches. Fasten off inside.

Making the Hanger

Pick up 4 stitches at the top of the hem at the back of the stocking. Work I-cord for 5" (for instructions on making I-cord, see We've Got Hang-Ups, page 77). Bind off and attach the bound-off end of the I-cord to the inside of the hem.

HEEL FLAP

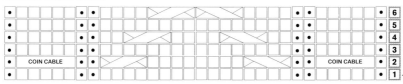

Row 4, Row 3, Row 2, Row 1

Start here

REINDEER AND BELLS

Rows 6, 5, 4, 3, 2 (COIN CABLE), 1

COIN CABLE

Pattern repeats twice

Start here →

KEY

☐	**Knit** on right side; purl on wrong side
•	**Purl** on right side; knit on wrong side
V	Slip 1 with yarn in back

C4R
Slip 2 to cable needle and hold in back, K2, knit stitches from cable needle

C4L
Slip 2 to cable needle and hold in front, K2, knit stitches from cable needle

Coin Cable
Slip 4 to cable needle and hold in back, K1, slip last 3 from cable needle back onto left-hand needle and bring the remaining stitch forward between the needles, keeping the yarn to the right of this stitch, K3 from left-hand needle, K1 from cable needle

Mock Cable
Knit into the second stitch on the left-hand needle and leave the stitch on the needle; knit into the first stitch, then drop both stitches off the needle.

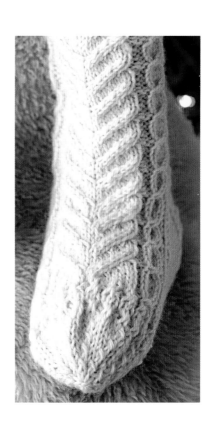

Pampered Pets

DESIGNED BY LOUISE SILVERMAN

Every family pet deserves his or her own stocking filled with special treats at the holidays. Customize these colorful knits by adding your pet's name in duplicate stitch in the band at the top after the stocking is completed. (See Alphabet chart, page 69.) This project features textural interest created by a few simple reverse-stockinette and slipped-stitch techniques.

FINISHED MEASUREMENTS

❋ 5½" wide x 16½" long

YARN

Cascade 220, 100% Peruvian Highland wool, worsted weight, 3½ oz (100 g)/220 yd (200 m) skeins

Kitten
MC	Garnet Heather (9341), 90 yds
CC A	Christmas Red (8895), 110 yds
CC B	Heather (2420), 80 yds
CC C	Mallard (2448), 70 yds

Puppy
MC	Yakima (9459), 90 yds
CC A	Peacock (2447), 110 yds
CC B	Marigold (7826), 80 yds
CC C	Provence (2425), 70 yds

NEEDLES

❋ One set of US 5 (3.75 mm) double-pointed needles *or size you need to obtain correct gauge*

❋ One US 5 (3.75 mm) circular needle, 16" long, *or size you need to obtain correct gauge*

GAUGE

❋ 22 stitches = 4" on US 5 (3.75 mm) needles in stockinette stitch

OTHER SUPPLIES

❋ Stitch markers, stitch holder, crochet hook, yarn needle

ABBREVIATIONS

CC	contrasting color		P	purl
K	knit		P2tog	purl 2 stitches together
K2tog	knit 2 stitches together		ssk	slip, slip, knit the 2 slipped stitches together
MC	main color			

Knitting the Cuff

SETUP: With circular needle and MC, cast on 60 stitches. Place a stitch marker on the needle and join into a round, taking care not to twist the stitches. (See Getting Around, page 16, for information about knitting in the round.)

NOTE: *All slipped stitches in the following rounds should be worked purlwise, with yarn at back.*

ROUNDS 1–6: Knit to the end of each round.

ROUND 7: Using CC A, *K1, slip 1; repeat from * to the end of the round.

ROUNDS 8 AND 9: Purl to the end of each round.

ROUND 10: Using CC B, *K1, slip 1; repeat from * to the end of the round.

ROUNDS 11 AND 12: Using CC A, purl to the end of each round.

ROUND 13: Using MC, *slip 1, K1; repeat from * to the end of the round.

ROUND 14: Purl to the end of the round.

ROUND 15: *K1, slip 1; repeat from * to the end of the round.

Knitting the Name Band

ROUNDS 1 AND 2: Using CC B, knit to the end of each round.

ROUND 3: *K2 with CC B, K2 with CC A; repeat from * to the end of the round. (See The Joy of Color, page 19, for information about multicolor, or stranded, knitting.)

ROUND 4: *K2 with CC B, P2 with CC A; repeat from * to the end of the round.

ROUNDS 5–16: Using CC B, knit to the end of each round.

ROUNDS 17 AND 18: Repeat rounds 3 and 4.

ROUNDS 19 AND 20: Using CC B, knit to the end of each round.

ROUND 21: Using MC, *K1, slip 1; repeat from * to the end of the round.

ROUNDS 22 AND 23: Purl to the end of each round.

ROUND 24: Using CC B, *slip 1, K1; repeat from * to the end of the round.

ROUND 25: Using MC, purl to the end of the round.

ROUND 26: Using CC A, *K1, slip 1; repeat from * to the end of the round.

Knitting the Pet Patterns

ROUNDS 1–13: Follow the Puppy Bone or Mouse chart (pages 50 and 51) for the color and stitch patterns. Begin where indicated on line 1 at the bottom of the chart and work from right to left, repeating the pattern four times around the stocking.

ROUND 14: Using MC, *K1, slip 1; repeat from * to the end of the round.

ROUND 15: Purl to the end of the round.

ROUND 16: Using CC B, *slip 1, K1; repeat from * to the end of the round.

ROUNDS 17–34: Follow the Tree chart on page 51 for color and stitch patterns. Begin where indicated on line 1 at bottom of chart and work from right to left, repeating the pattern six times around stocking. Note that some interesting texture is created by purl stitches as indicated on chart.

ROUND 35: Using MC, *K1, slip 1; repeat from * to the end of the round.

ROUND 36: Purl to the end of the round.

ROUND 37: Using CC A, *slip 1, K1; repeat from * to the end of the round.

ROUNDS 38 AND 39: Knit to the end of each round.

Making the Heel Flap

SETUP: Using CC A, K14, place the next 32 stitches on a stitch holder.

You now have 28 stitches left on the needle.

With CC C, work flat (back and forth on the circular needles) on the remaining stitches to make the heel flap, turning after each row.

ROW 1 (WRONG SIDE): Slip 1, P27.

ROW 2 (RIGHT SIDE): *Slip 1, K1; repeat from * to end of row.

ROWS 3–20: Repeat rows 1 and 2.

Turning the Heel

ROW 1: Slip 1, P15, P2tog, P1, turn. (*9 stitches remain unworked on needle.*)

ROW 2: Slip 1, K5, ssk, K1, turn. (*9 stitches remain unworked on needle.*)

ROW 3: Slip 1, purl until 1 stitch remains before the gap formed by the last turning, P2tog, P1, turn.

ROW 4: Slip 1, knit until 1 stitch remains before the gap, ssk, K1, turn.

ROWS 5–12: Repeat rows 3 and 4, working in stockinette stitch, slipping the first stitch and decreasing 1 stitch to bridge the gap until you have worked all stitches, and 16 stitches remain on the needle. End with a knit row. This is the bottom of the heel.

Knitting the Instep

SETUP: Using CC A, knit the 32 stitches from the stitch holder, pick up and K11 from the left-hand side of the heel, K8 from the bottom of the heel, place a stitch marker to indicate the beginning of the round, K8 remaining stitches from the bottom of the heel, and pick up and K11 from the right-hand side of the heel. (See Picking Up Stitches, page 92.)

You now have 70 stitches on the needle.

Knit to the stitch marker to begin the next round.

ROUND 1: K16, K2tog, place stitch marker, K34, place stitch marker, ssk, K16.

You now have 68 stitches.

ROUNDS 2, 4, 6, AND 8: Knit to the end of each round.

ROUND 3: Knit until 2 stitches remain before the first stitch marker, K2tog, knit to the next stitch marker, ssk, knit to the end of the round.

You now have 66 stitches.

ROUNDS 5, 7, AND 9: Continue in the same manner as round 3, decreasing 2 stitches every other round, keeping 34 stitches between the decreases, until you have 60 stitches.

Remove the two stitch markers for the decreases, leaving the stitch marker at the beginning of the round.

Knitting the Foot

Follow appropriate paw chart (page 50 or 51) for color and stitch patterns. Begin where indicated on line 1 at the bottom of the chart and work from right to left, repeating the pattern six times around the stocking. Work the Puppy Paws chart from rounds 1–21; work the Kitten Paws chart from rounds 1–16, then repeat rounds 1–6.

NEXT 3 ROUNDS: With CC A, knit to the end of each round.

Shaping the Toe

ROUND 1: Using CC C, K13, K2tog, place stitch marker, ssk, K26, K2tog, place stitch marker, ssk, K13. *You now have* 56 stitches.

ROUNDS 2–10: Continue in stockinette stitch, working K2tog before and ssk after each stitch marker. Change to double-pointed needles when necessary.

At the end of round 10, *you now have* 20 stitches.

ROUND 11: Knit to the first stitch marker. Place the next 10 stitches on one double-pointed needle and the remaining 10 stitches on another double-pointed needle.

Cut yarn, leaving a 24" tail, and graft the two sides together with the tail, using Kitchener stitch. (See Kitchener Stitch on page 93.)

Finishing

Cut yarn and thread it through a yarn needle. Weave in all loose ends.

Work the desired name in the name band with Duplicate Stitch (see page 111), using the Alphabet chart on page 69 for guidance.

Make a 6" hanger following the instructions for Twisted Bundles, page 91.

KEY FOR KITTEN CHARTS

MC   Garnet Heather

CC A   Christmas Red

CC B   Heather

CC C   Mallard

[O] purl on right side

[O] purl on right side

[O] purl on right side

MOUSE

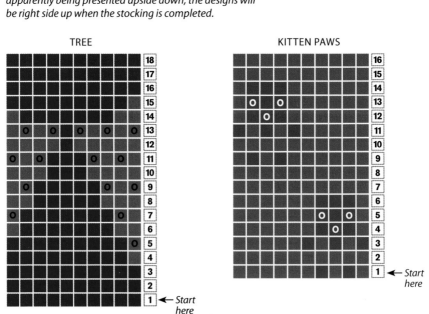

Note: *It is customary in knitting books for charts to be followed from bottom to top, and, when knitting circularly, from right to left. Although this results in some charts apparently being presented upside down, the designs will be right side up when the stocking is completed.*

TREE

KITTEN PAWS

KEY FOR PUPPY CHARTS

■	MC	Yakima
■	CC A	Peacock
■	CC C	Marigold
■	CC C	Provence
O	purl on right side	

PUPPY BONE

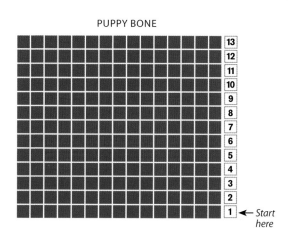

← Start here

PUPPY PAWS

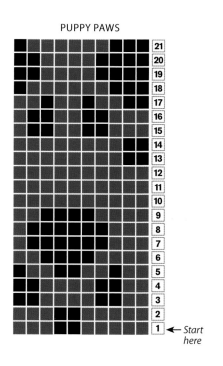

← Start here

TREE

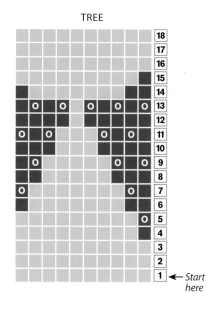

← Start here

51

Christmas Sampler

DESIGNED BY GWEN STEEGE

Who said that monochromatic color schemes are dull? In this fiery-bright worsted-wool stocking, three shades of red, sparked by delicate lines of white, let you show off nine different color combinations.

FINISHED MEASUREMENTS

※ 6½" wide x 22" long

YARN

Brown Sheep Nature Spun, 100% wool, worsted weight, 3½ oz (100 g)/245 yd (224 m) skeins

MC	Red Fox, 2 skeins
CC A	Scarlet, 2 skeins
CC B	Brick Road, 1 skein
CC C	Snow, 1 skein

NEEDLES

※ One set of US 7 (4.5 mm) double-pointed needles *or size you need to obtain correct gauge*

GAUGE

※ 22 stitches = 4" on US 7 (4.5 mm) needles in any Flame Band pattern stitch

OTHER SUPPLIES

※ Stitch marker, stitch holder, I-9 (5.5 mm) crochet hook, yarn needle

ABBREVIATIONS

CC	contrasting color		P	purl
K	knit		P2tog	purl 2 stitches together
K2tog	knit 2 stitches together		ssk	slip, slip, knit the 2 slipped stitches together
MC	main color			

Knitting the Cuff and Leg

SETUP: With double-pointed needles and MC, cast on 72 stitches.

Knit the first 18 stitches onto Needle 1. Knit the next 18 stitches onto Needle 2. Knit the next 18 stitches onto Needle 3. Slide the remaining 18 stitches onto Needle 1 with the first 18 stitches, and knit to where you began.

You now have on

    Needle 1: 36 stitches

    Needle 2: 18 stitches

    Needle 3: 18 stitches

NOTE: *The beginning of each round will be at the center back, which is in the middle of Needle 1. Place a stitch marker to help you keep track. As you begin round 1, be sure the stitches aren't twisted around the needle anywhere.*

ROUNDS 1 AND 3: Purl to the end of each round.

At the end of round 3, *you now have* 2 garter-stitch ridges.

ROUND 2: Knit to the end of the round.

ROUND 4: Using CC C, knit to the end of the round. Join CC A.

ROUNDS 5–14: *K2 with CC A, K2 with MC; repeat from * to the end of each round.

ROUND 15: Using CC C, knit to the end of the round.

ROUND 16: Using MC, knit to the end of the round.

ROUNDS 17–19: Repeat rounds 1–3.

At the end of round 19, *you now have* 2 garter-stitch ridges.

ROUNDS 20–91: Work the charts for the Flame Bands on page 59. Begin where indicated on line 1 at the bottom right of each chart. Work charts in this order: 1, 2, 3, 4, 1, 4, 3, 2, 1 (nine color bands in all). For advice about working with two colors, see The Joy of Color, page 19.

ROUND 92: Using CC C, knit to end of round. Break off CC C.

Making the Heel Flap

SETUP: Place stitches from Needles 2 and 3 on a stitch holder. Slip the remaining 36 stitches onto one needle. Join MC. You will be working these 36 stitches back and forth in rows on two needles to knit the heel.

ROW 1 (RIGHT SIDE): Using MC, *slip 1, K1; repeat from * to the end of the row.

ROW 2 (WRONG SIDE): Slip 1, purl to the end of the row.

NEXT ROWS: Repeat rows 1 and 2 until work measures 3", ending with a purl row.

Turning the Heel

ROW 1: Slip 1, K18, ssk, K1, turn. (*14 stitches remain unworked on needle.*)

ROW 2: Slip 1, P3, P2tog, P1, turn. (*14 stitches remain unworked on needle.*)

ROW 3: Slip 1, K4, ssk, K1, turn. (*12 stitches remain unworked on needle.*)

ROW 4: Slip 1, P5, P2tog, P1, turn. (*12 stitches remain unworked on needle.*)

NEXT ROWS: Continue to work the pattern as established, knitting or purling together the 2 stitches on each side of the gap formed in the previous row until you have worked all the stitches in the row. End with a purl row.

You now have 20 stitches.

Knitting the Instep

SETUP: Redistribute the stitches as follows: Divide the 20 heel stitches by placing 10 stitches on Needle 1 and 10 stitches on Needle 3. Slide the 36 stitches from the holder (instep stitches) onto Needle 2. Break the yarn and join it again at the beginning of Needle 1.

ROUND 1:

Needle 1: With MC, knit the 10 stitches on the needle, then pick up and knit 18 stitches from along the left-hand side of the heel. (See Picking Up Stitches, page 92.)

Needle 2: Knit to the end of the needle.

Needle 3: Using an empty needle, pick up and knit 18 stitches along the right-hand side of the heel, then knit the remaining 10 stitches from Needle 3.
You now have a total of 92 stitches.

ROUND 2 (WITH MC ONLY):

> **Needle 1:** Knit to the last 3 stitches on the needle, K2tog, K1.
> *You now have 27 stitches on Needle 1.*
>
> **Needle 2:** K1, ssk, knit to the last 3 stitches on the needle, K2tog, K1.
> *You now have 34 stitches on Needle 2.*
>
> **Needle 3:** K1, ssk, knit to the end of the needle.
> *You now have 27 stitches on Needle 3.*

NOTE: *In the following rounds, you will be following the Sampler charts on page 59, and at the same time decreasing at the end of Needle 1 and at the beginning of Needle 3 every other row to form the gusset. The decreases at the beginning of Needle 3 will affect the color order that follows. Be sure to keep CC A stitches in a vertical line throughout the section. Drop CC A on the even-numbered rounds, where it is not used.*

ROUND 3:

> **Needle 1:** *K1 with CC A, K1 with MC; repeat from * to the last 2 stitches, K2 with MC. (Refer to Sampler 1 on page 59 for the stitch pattern.)
>
> **Needle 2:** *K2 with CC A, K2 with MC; repeat from * to the end of the needle, ending K2 with CC A. (Refer to Sampler 2 on page 59 for the stitch pattern.)
>
> **Needle 3:** K2 with MC, *K1 with MC, K1 with CC A; repeat from * to the end of the needle.

ROUND 4 (WITH MC ONLY):

> **Needle 1:** Knit to the last 3 stitches, K2tog, K1.
>
> **Needle 2:** Knit to the end of the needle.
>
> **Needle 3:** K1, ssk, knit to the end of the needle.

ROUNDS 5–22: Repeat rounds 3 and 4. In odd-numbered rows, maintain 2 MC stitches at the end of Needle 1 and the beginning of Needle 3. In even-numbered rows, knit with MC only.

At the end of round 22, *you now have* 17 stitches remaining on Needles 1 and 3 and 34 stitches on Needle 2, for a total of 68 stitches.

Completing the Foot

NOTE: *Refer to Sampler Stripe chart on page 59 for color pattern on Needles 1 and 3, and Sampler Checkerboard chart for color pattern on Needle 2 in this section.*

ROUNDS 1 AND 2:

> **Needle 1:** *K1 with CC A, K1 with MC; repeat from * to the last stitch, K1 with MC.
>
> **Needle 2:** *K2 with CC A, K2 with MC; repeat from * to the last 2 stitches, K2 with CC A.
>
> **Needle 3:** K2 with MC, *K1 with MC, K1 with CC A; repeat from * to the last stitch, K1 with MC.

ROUNDS 3 AND 4:

> **Needle 1:** *K1 with CC A, K1 with MC; repeat from * to the last stitch, K1 with MC.
>
> **Needle 2:** *K2 with MC, K2 with CC A; repeat from * to the last 2 stitches, K2 with MC.
>
> **Needle 3:** K2 with MC, *K1 with MC, K1 with CC A; repeat from * to the last stitch, K1 with MC.

NEXT ROUNDS: Repeat rounds 1–4 until work measures 5" from the back of the heel.

Shaping the Toe

ROUND 1:

> **Needle 1:** Using MC, knit to the last 3 stitches, K2tog, K1.
> *You now have* 16 stitches on the needle.
>
> **Needle 2:** Knit to the end of the needle.
>
> **Needle 3:** K1, ssk, knit to the end of the needle.
> *You now have* 16 stitches on the needle.

ROUNDS 2–9: Work Flame Band 2 on page 59.

ROUND 10: Change to CC C, and knit to the end of the round. Cut CC C, and join MC.

ROUND 11:

> **Needle 1:** Knit to the end of the needle.
> *You now have* 16 stitches on the needle.
>
> **Needle 2:** K1, ssk, knit to the last 3 stitches, K2tog, K1.
> *You now have* 32 stitches on the needle.
>
> **Needle 3:** Knit to the end of the needle.
> *You now have* 16 stitches on the needle.

ROUND 12: Knit to the end of the round.

ROUND 13:

> **Needle 1:** Knit to the last 3 stitches, K2tog, K1.
>
> **Needle 2:** K1, ssk, knit to last 3 stitches, K2tog, K1.
>
> **Needle 3:** K1, ssk, knit to end of needle.

NEXT ROUNDS: Repeat rounds 12 and 13 until 16 stitches remain (4 stitches on Needles 1 and 3, and 8 stitches on Needle 2).

Knit the stitches from Needle 1 onto Needle 3. Use Kitchener stitch (see page 93) to graft the remaining toe stitches together.

Making the Hanger and Tassel

For the hanger, you need one 10" I-cord in each of the following colors: MC, CC A, and CC B. For the tassel, you need one 7" I-cord in each of the same colors. Using 3 cast-on stitches, follow directions for making I-cord on page 77.

The hanger:
Braid the three 10" I-cords together, then use a crochet hook to pull the braid through the stocking at the back, just below the top garter-stitch band. Make an overhand knot to secure the braids into a loop.

The tassel:
Braid the three 7" I-cords together, then use a crochet hook to pull the braid through the toe of the stocking at the very tip. Tie an overhand knot on the inside to secure the braid. Take three 10" lengths of MC, CC A, and CC C yarns, and wrap them several times around the braid about 1½" from the end to secure it. Tie overhand knots at the end of each separate I-cord on the outside.

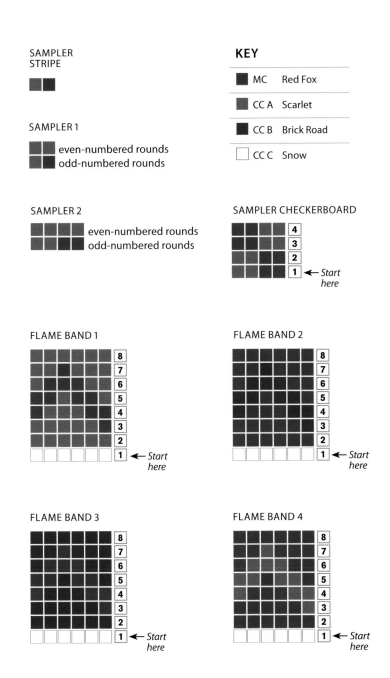

SAMPLER
STRIPE

SAMPLER 1

even-numbered rounds
odd-numbered rounds

SAMPLER 2

even-numbered rounds
odd-numbered rounds

KEY

MC   Red Fox

CC A   Scarlet

CC B   Brick Road

CC C   Snow

SAMPLER CHECKERBOARD

4
3
2
1 ← *Start here*

FLAME BAND 1

8
7
6
5
4
3
2
1 ← *Start here*

FLAME BAND 2

8
7
6
5
4
3
2
1 ← *Start here*

FLAME BAND 3

8
7
6
5
4
3
2
1 ← *Start here*

FLAME BAND 4

8
7
6
5
4
3
2
1 ← *Start here*

Mix-and-Match Stockings

DESIGNED BY NANCY LINDBERG

With 17 different patterns for you to mix and match, you can knit a unique stocking for everyone in the family. The "afterthought heel" lets you knit straight to the toe and then add the heel afterward. We offer directions for both worsted- (shown) and bulky-weight versions of this stocking.

FINISHED MEASUREMENTS

❋ 7" wide × 22½" long

Worsted-Weight Version

YARN

Brown Sheep Lamb's Pride, 100% wool, worsted weight, 4 oz (113 g)/190 yd (173 m) skeins

MC	Sandy Heather (M-01),	175 yds
CC A	Old Sage (M-69),	90 yds
CC B	Chianti (M-28),	90 yds
CC C	Amethyst (M-62),	90 yds
CC D	Cream (M-10),	90 yds

NEEDLES

❋ One US 8 (5 mm) circular needle, 16" long, *or size you need to obtain correct gauge*

GAUGE

❋ 20 stitches = 4" on US 8 (5 mm) needles in stockinette stitch

Bulky-Weight Version

YARN

MC	150 yds	**CC C**	70 yds
CC A	70 yds	**CC D**	70 yds
CC B	70 yds		

NEEDLES

❋ One US 9 (5.5 mm) circular needle, 16" long, *or size you need to obtain correct gauge*

GAUGE

❋ 16 stitches = 4" on US 9 (5.5 mm) needles in stockinette stitch

OTHER SUPPLIES

❋ Stitch markers, small quantity of scrap yarn in similar weight but different color, crochet hook, yarn needle

ABBREVIATIONS	
CC	contrasting color
K	knit
K2tog	knit 2 stitches together
MC	main color
P	purl
ssk	slip, slip, knit the 2 slipped stitches together
st(s)	stitch(es)

Knitting the Cuff

	WORSTED	BULKY
With MC, using the circular needle, cast on	72 sts	60 sts

Join the yarn to work in the round, taking care not to twist the stitches. Place a stitch marker between the last and first cast-on stitches to mark the beginning of the round. (See Getting Around, page 16, for information about knitting in the round.)

Work in K2, P2 ribbing for 1½".

Making the Name Band

ROUND 1: With MC, knit to the end of the round.

ROUNDS 2–4: Using MC and CC A, knit to the end of each round, following the Chain chart on page 65 for color pattern. Begin where indicated on line 1 at the bottom of the chart and work from right to left, repeating the pattern to the end of the round. Carry unused colors loosely behind work. (For more information about multicolor knitting, see The Joy of Color, page 19.)

ROUNDS 5–15: Using MC, knit to the end of each round. (If desired, the name will be added in these rounds later.)

ROUNDS 16–18: Repeat rounds 2–4.

ROUND 19: With MC, knit to the end of the round.

Knitting the Leg

Select an assortment of patterns from the Mix-and-Match charts on pages 65–68. For each pattern, Begin where indicated on line 1 at the bottom of the chart and work from right to left, repeating each pattern until the end of the round. Do not cut the yarn until you reach a round where that color is no longer used.

	WORSTED	BULKY
Using selected patterns, work even in stockinette stitch for	10"–11"	9½"–10"

Marking for the Heel

	WORSTED	BULKY
Cut the yarn. Slide onto the left-hand needle the last	18 sts	15 sts
Join scrap yarn of a different color and	K36	K30
Cut the scrap yarn.		

Knitting the Foot

NOTE: *For the rest of the piece, start the rounds with the first stitch after the scrap yarn. Move the stitch marker to this position.*

Select patterns from the Mix-and-Match charts. For each pattern, begin where indicated on line 1 at bottom of the chart and work from right to left, repeating each pattern until the end of the round.

Using selected patterns, work even in stockinette stitch for 4"–5".

Shaping the Toe

	WORSTED	BULKY
ROUND 1: With MC,	K36	K30
Place a marker indicating the halfway point, and continue knitting to 3 stitches before the end of the round, K2tog, K1, slip marker.		
You now have	71 sts	59 sts
ROUND 2: K1, ssk, knit to 3 stitches before the halfway marker, K2tog, K1, slip marker, K1, ssk, knit to the end of the round.		
You now have	68 sts	56 sts
ROUND 3: Knit to 3 stitches before the end of the round, K2tog, K1.		
You now have	67 sts	55 sts
NEXT ROUNDS: Repeat rounds 2 and 3	6 times	5 times
LAST ROUND: Repeat round 2. *You now have*	40 sts	32 sts

Cut yarn, leaving a 36" tail.

Divide stitches equally, sliding half of the stitches to each end of the circular needles. Graft the toe with Kitchener stitch. (See Kitchener Stitch, page 93.)

Making the Afterthought Heel

Carefully pull out the scrap yarn and place the live stitches from the rows above and below the scrap yarn on a circular needle. Place stitch markers where the stitches split between the upper and lower rows.

Join MC after one of the stitch markers.

Using MC, shape and finish the heel just as you did the toe.

Making the Loop

At the center back of the top of the sock, pick up and knit 3 stitches (see Picking Up Stitches, page 92).

Knit a 3" I-cord, following We've Got Hang-Ups instructions on page 77.

Tie off the I-cord and tack the end to the beginning of the I-cord, making a loop.

Finishing

With a yarn needle and Duplicate Stitch (see page 111), work the name of the stocking's owner into the name band, using the Alphabet chart on page 69 for guidance. Center the words on the band, and leave a stitch between each letter. You can probably fit the name twice, on the front and on the back. Using the same method, work the year into the sock's toe.

Cut the yarn and weave in all loose ends on wrong side of work.

MIX-AND-MATCH CHARTS

The charts and color key on this and the next page are those used in the stocking pictured on page 61. You will find more designs on the following pages. Color choices are entirely yours!

Note: *It's customary in knitting books for charts to be followed from bottom to top, and, when knitting circularly, from right to left. Although this results in some charts apparently being presented upside down, the designs will be right side up when the stocking is completed, because you're knitting from the top.*

KEY

▨	MC	Sandy Heather
▨	CC A	Old Sage
▨	CC B	Chianti
▨	CC C	Amethyst
☐	CC D	Cream

ZIGZAG

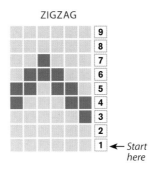

← Start here

HOLLY

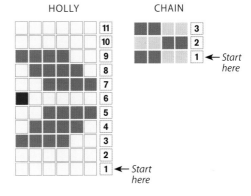

← Start here

CHAIN

← Start here

CHRISTMAS TREE

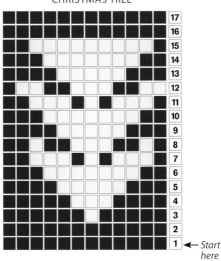

← Start here

WREATH

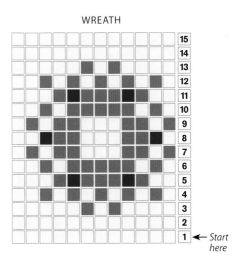

← Start here

REINDEER

BOY

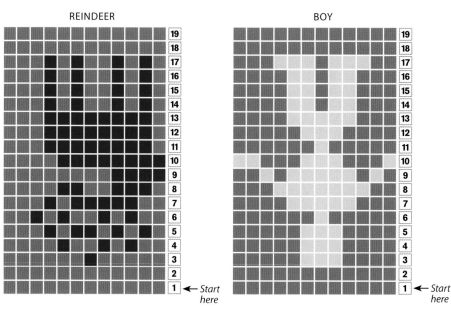

ELF

GIRL

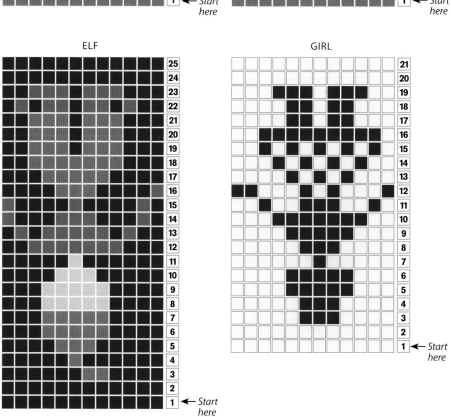

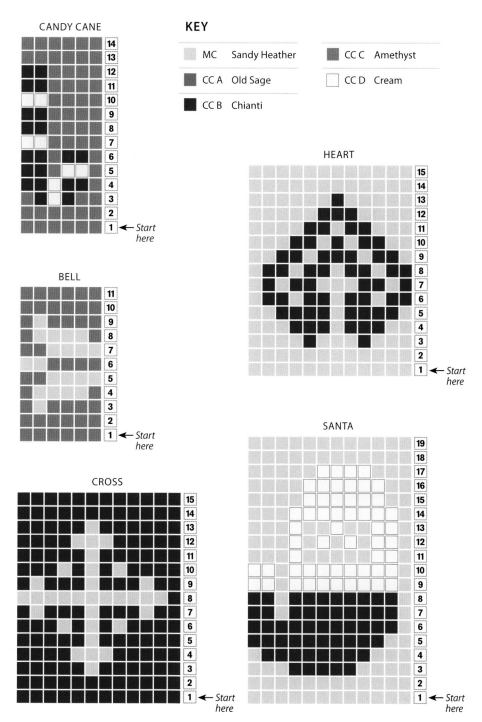

CANDY CANE

BELL

CROSS

KEY

	MC	Sandy Heather		CC C	Amethyst
	CC A	Old Sage		CC D	Cream
	CC B	Chianti			

HEART

SANTA

Start here

67

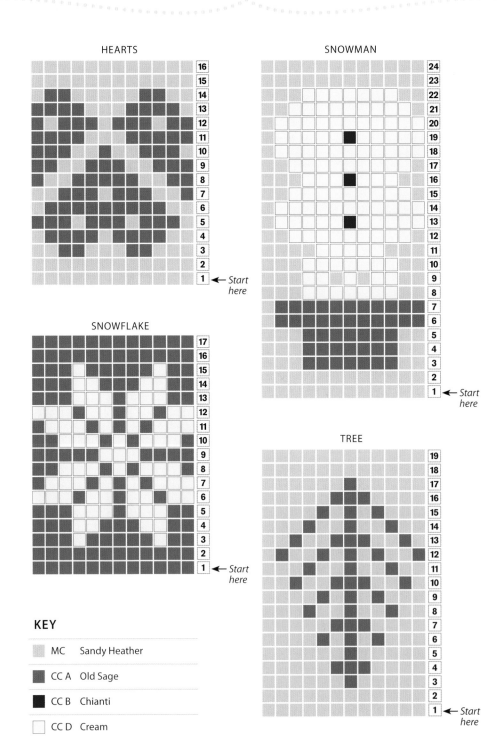

HEARTS

SNOWMAN

SNOWFLAKE

TREE

KEY

	MC	Sandy Heather
	CC A	Old Sage
	CC B	Chianti
	CC D	Cream

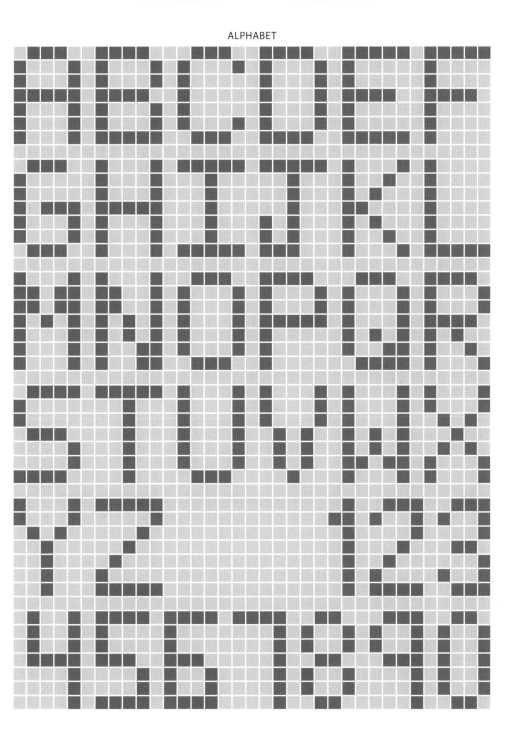

Jester's Bells

DESIGNED BY LYNDA GEMMELL

The jester stripes and bells that were traditional wear for the "motley fool" in centuries past still have the power to charm us today. This extra-roomy stocking features textural interest in its garter-stitch cuff and garter-stitch bands on the heel and toe. You'll enjoy the slightly different technique for knitting the stocking heel.

FINISHED MEASUREMENTS

❋ 8½" wide x 20½" long

YARN

Green Mountain Spinnery Mountain Mohair, 30% mohair/70% wool, worsted weight, 2 oz (57 g)/140 yd (128 m) skeins

MC	Periwinkle Blue (7367), 1 skein	
CC A	Coral Bell (7136), 1 skein	
CC B	Maritime (7622), 1 skein	

ABBREVIATIONS

CC	contrasting color
K	knit
K2tog	knit 2 stitches together
MC	main color
P	purl
P2tog	purl 2 stitches together
ssk	slip, slip, knit the 2 slipped stitches together

NEEDLES

❋ One set of US 9 (5.5 mm) double-pointed needles *or size you need to obtain correct gauge*

❋ One US 9 (5.5 mm) circular needle, 16" long, *or size you need to obtain correct gauge*

GAUGE

❋ 17 stitches = 4" on US 9 (5.5 mm) needles in stockinette stitch

OTHER SUPPLIES

❋ Stitch markers, crochet hook, yarn needle, twelve ½" jingle bells

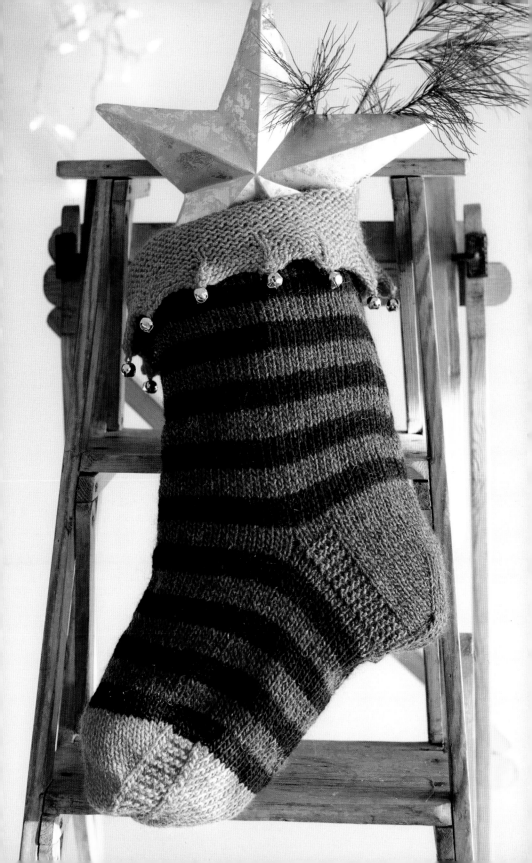

Knitting the Cuff

NOTE: *In this section, work back and forth on a circular needle, turning after each row. See Double Decrease, page 73, for advice on the decreases in rows 2, 4, and 6.*

SETUP: Using CC A and circular needle, cast on 144 stitches.

ROW 1 (WRONG SIDE): Knit to the end of the row.

ROW 2: K4, *Double Decrease, K9; repeat from * 10 more times; Double Decrease, K5. *You now have* 120 stitches.

ROW 3: K5, *P1, K9; repeat from * 10 more times; P1, K4.

ROW 4: K3, *Double Decrease, K7; repeat from * 10 more times; Double Decrease, K4. *You now have* 96 stitches.

ROW 5: K4, *P1, K7; repeat from * 10 more times; P1, K3.

ROW 6: K2, *Double Decrease, K5; repeat from * 10 more times; Double Decrease, K3. *You now have* 72 stitches.

ROW 7: K3, *P1, K5; repeat from * 10 more times; P1, K2.

ROW 8: Knit to the end of the row.

ROWS 9 AND 10: Repeat rows 7 and 8.

NEXT ROWS: Continue in garter stitch (knit every row) until the cuff measures 4", measuring at a jester point (where the decreases were made).

TURNING ROW (RIGHT SIDE): Purl to the end of the row. This row is where you will turn the cuff when the stocking is completed. Continue knitting in garter stitch until the cuff measures 6", measuring at a jester point.

Knitting the Leg

SETUP: With the wrong side of the cuff facing you, join the stocking into a round. (Identify the right side by the line of stockinette stitches at each point.)

NOTE: *To make a smooth transition from one color to the next, as you change yarn colors in the stripes in this section, break the yarn at the end of every stripe and leave the tails on the inside. When the stocking is completed, sew in the loose ends on the diagonal, as described and illustrated on page 20. The tails from the beginning of the stripes are sewn up and to the left, while the tails from the end of the stripes are sewn down and to the right. This trick gets rid of the jog where a new color starts.*

ROUND 1: Still using CC A, knit to the end of the round. Cut CC A.

ROUNDS 2–6: Using MC, knit.

ROUNDS 7–11: Using CC B, knit.

ROUNDS 12–51: Repeat the stripe pattern as in rounds 2–11.
You now have five MC stripes and five CC B stripes.

ROUNDS 52 AND 53: Change to MC, and knit, stopping at the end of the round (center back of stocking).

DOUBLE DECREASE

Decrease 2 stitches in 1 stitch, as follows: slip 2 stitches together as if to knit, knit the next stitch (a), pass the 2 slipped stitches over the just-knit stitch (b).

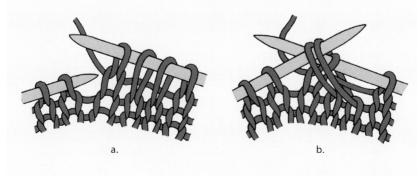

a.   b.

Making the Heel Flap

SETUP ROW 1: With MC, K18 onto a double-pointed needle.

SETUP ROW 2: Turn the work, purl the 18 stitches you just knitted, and then purl an additional 18 stitches.

Work these 36 stitches on two double-pointed needles, turning after each row, as follows:

* ❉ **ROW 1 (RIGHT SIDE):** K36.
* ❉ **ROW 2 (WRONG SIDE):** K5, P26, K5.
* ❉ **ROWS 3–16:** Repeat rows 1 and 2.

You now have 8 garter-stitch ridges at the edge of the heel flap. This is a modified box heel, which sits nice and flat for a stocking.

Turning the Heel

ROW 1 (RIGHT SIDE): K13, K2tog, K6, ssk, K13.

You now have 34 stitches.

ROWS 2, 4, 6, 8, AND 10 (WRONG SIDE): K5, purl to the last 5 stitches, K5.

ROW 3: K12, K2tog, K6, ssk, K12.

You now have 32 stitches.

ROW 5: K11, K2tog, K6, ssk, K11.

You now have 30 stitches.

ROW 7: K10, K2tog, K6, ssk, K10.

You now have 28 stitches.

ROW 9: K9, K2tog, K6, ssk, K9.

You now have 26 stitches.

ROW 11: K16, ssk. Turn.

ROW 12: Slip 1, P6, P2tog. Turn.

ROW 13: Slip 1, K6, ssk. Turn.

ROW 14: Slip 1, P6, P2tog. Turn.

ROWS 15–28: Repeat rows 13 and 14. All side stitches are used, and 8 stitches remain.

Knitting the Foot

SETUP: Continuing to use MC, K4 onto the circular needle. Place a stitch marker to mark the center of the heel. All rounds now begin here.

NOTE: *For information about how to pick up stitches along the heel, see Picking Up Stitches on page 92.*

ROUND 1:

- ❋ With the circular needle, K4. (Leave the 36 stitches for the instep in place on the circular needle.)
- ❋ Pick up and knit 13 stitches by knitting into 13 ridges down the left-hand side of the heel flap.
- ❋ Pick up and K1 in the corner to close the gap.
- ❋ K36 across the instep stitches already on the circular needle.
- ❋ Pick up and K1 in the corner.
- ❋ Pick up and knit 13 stitches by knitting into the ridges on the right-hand side of the heel flap.
- ❋ K4 to the center of the heel.

You now have 72 stitches.

ROUNDS 2 AND 3: Using MC, knit to the end of each round.

ROUNDS 4–8: Using CC B, knit to the end of each round.

ROUNDS 9–13: Using MC, knit to the end of each round.

NEXT ROUNDS: Repeat rounds 4–13 (stripe pattern) until the foot measures 6" from the end of the heel flap (where you resumed knitting in the round). Finish the stripe you are working on. Cut both yarns.

Shaping the Toe

ROUND 1: Using CC A, knit 18 stitches onto each of four double-pointed needles.

ROUND 2:

>   **Needle 1:** Knit to the last 4 stitches, K2tog, P2.
>   **Needle 2:** P2, ssk, knit to the end of the needle.
>   **Needle 3:** Knit to the last 4 stitches, K2tog, P2.
>   **Needle 4:** P2, ssk, knit to the end of the round.

You now have 68 stitches.

ROUND 3: Knit to the end of the round.

ROUNDS 4–19: Repeat rounds 2 and 3.

You now have 36 stitches.

ROUND 20: Repeat round 2.

ROUND 21:

    Needle 1: Knit to the last 4 stitches, K2tog, K2.

    Needle 2: K2, ssk, knit to the end of the needle.

    Needle 3: Knit to the last 4 stitches, K2tog, K2.

    Needle 4: K2, ssk, knit to the end of the round.

ROUNDS 22–25: Repeat rounds 20 and 21.

You now have 12 stitches.

Finishing

Cut yarn, leaving a 12" tail. Thread the tail through a yarn needle, draw through remaining stitches, and pull tight. Weave in all loose ends on the wrong side of the work.

Stitch the seam in the garter-stitch cuff with the right sides of the cuff facing each other. Weave in the cast-on tail so it won't show when the cuff is turned down. Turn the cuff down along the Turning Row (a purl row; see page 72).

Using matching yarn and a yarn needle, sew a jingle bell onto the cuff at each of the 12 points.

THE HANGING LOOP: Using CC B, cast on 3 stitches and make a 4" I-cord (see We've Got Hang-Ups at right for instructions). Bind off. Fold the loop in half and stitch it to the inside of the cuff.

WE'VE GOT HANG-UPS

We want no weak hangers when we're packing our stockings full of goodies, so our designers have offered a variety of styles, including those shown
below (clockwise, from left): stockinette-stitch loop; I-Cord (instructions follow);
Braided I-Cord (page 58); braid; crocheted loop; Twisted Bundles (page 91).

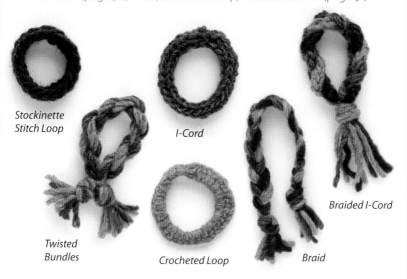

Stockinette
Stitch Loop

I-Cord

Braided I-Cord

Twisted
Bundles

Crocheted Loop

Braid

To make I-cord:

Step 1. Using double-pointed needles, cast on 2, 3, or 4 stitches (as the pattern directs); knit all stitches.

Step 2. Do not turn the needle. Instead, slide
the stitches to the right-hand end of
the needle, so the first cast-on stitch
is the first stitch at the tip of the left-
hand needle and the last stitch knitted
is farthest away from the tip. Insert the
right-hand needle knitwise into that
stitch, bring the yarn across the back of
the piece, and use it to knit as usual.

STEP 2

Step 3. Knit the remaining stitches on the needle.

Step 4. Repeat steps 2 and 3 to desired length.

Star Brocade

DESIGNED BY EVELYN A. CLARK

Seed-stitch stars are scattered across a stockinette-stitch background on this elegant stocking. You can choose between a straight edge or a scalloped edge (shown opposite) for the top. The stocking also features a seed-stitch band in a contrasting color, an easy short-row heel, and a round, gathered toe.

FINISHED MEASUREMENTS

※ 7¾" wide x 21" long

YARN

MC Plymouth Select, 100% superwash Merino, worsted weight, 3½ oz (100 g)/ 218 yd (200 m), Natural, 2 skeins

CC Zealana Aspire's Heron, 80% Merino/ 20% possum, worsted weight, 1.75 oz (50 g)/109 yd (100 m), Cloud Blue (H01), 1 skein

NEEDLES

※ One US 6 (4 mm) circular needle, 16" long, *or size you need to obtain correct gauge*

※ One set of US 6 (4 mm) double-pointed needles *or size you need to obtain correct gauge*

GAUGE

※ 20 stitches = 4" on US 6 (4 mm) needles in pattern stitch

OTHER SUPPLIES

※ Stitch marker, yarn needle

ABBREVIATIONS

CC	contrasting color	psso	pass slipped stitch over
K	knit	ssk	slip, slip, knit the 2 slipped stitches together
K2tog	knit 2 stitches together		
MC	main color	W&T	wrap and turn
P	purl	yo	yarn over

Knitting the Cuff

Scallop-Top Version (shown)

SETUP: With circular needle and MC, cast on 80 stitches.

Place stitch marker on the needle and join into a round, taking care not to twist the stitches. (See Getting Around, page 16, for information about knitting in the round.)

ROUND 1: Purl to the end of the round.

ROUND 2: *K1, yo, K2, slip 1 knitwise, K2tog, psso, K2, yo; repeat from * to the end of the round.

ROUNDS 3 AND 5: Knit to the end of each round.

ROUND 4: *K2, yo, K1, slip 1 knitwise, K2tog, psso, K1, yo, K1; repeat from * to the end of the round.

ROUND 6: *K3, yo, slip 1 knitwise, K2tog, psso, yo, K2; repeat from * to the end of the round.

ROUND 7: *K38, K2tog; repeat from * to the end of the round.

You now have 78 stitches.

Straight-Top Version

SETUP: With circular needle and using CC, cast on 78 stitches.

Place a stitch marker on the needle and join into a round, taking care not to twist the stitches.

Knitting the Seed-Stitch Band

ROUNDS 1 AND 3: Using CC, knit to the end of each round.

ROUND 2: Purl to the end of the round.

ROUNDS 4, 6, AND 8: *P1, K1; repeat from * to the end of each round.

ROUNDS 5 AND 7: *K1, P1; repeat from * to the end of each round.

ROUND 9: Knit to the end of the round.

ROUND 10: Purl to the end of the round. Break off CC yarn.

Knitting the Star Brocade

ROUNDS 1–70: Using MC, follow Star 1 chart on page 84 for the stitch pattern. Begin with line 1 at bottom of chart and work from right to left, repeating the pattern three times around the stocking. Work Lines 1–22 once, then repeat Lines 7–22 three more times.

Shaping the Top of the Heel

SETUP: Slip the stitch marker, slip and wrap the first stitch, place both the marker and the stitch back on the left needle, and turn the work (see Wrap & Turn, page 9). The heel is worked flat on short rows, turning after each row; the rest of the stitches can stay on the needle, but you won't need them again until the heel is finished.

You will be working a single star pattern while shaping the heel. Follow Star 2 chart on page 85 for the stitch pattern where indicated, starting at the bottom with line 1 and working from left to right. Remember that you are now working flat, so wrong-side rows are worked from left to right, with knits and purls reversed. Since you are starting with a wrong-side row, begin at the left of the chart.

ROW 1 (WRONG SIDE): P13, Star 2 chart, P13, W&T.

ROW 2 (RIGHT SIDE): K13, Star 2 chart, K12, W&T.

ROW 3: P12, Star 2 chart, P12, W&T.

ROW 4: K12, Star 2 chart, K11, W&T.

ROW 5: P11, Star 2 chart, P11, W&T.

ROW 6: K11, Star 2 chart, K10, W&T.

ROW 7: P10, Star 2 chart, P10, W&T.

ROW 8: K10, Star 2 chart, K9, W&T.

ROW 9: P9, Star 2 chart, P9, W&T.

ROW 10: K9, Star 2 chart, K8, W&T.

ROW 11: P29, W&T.

ROW 12: K28, W&T.

Continue in stockinette stitch, working on 1 fewer stitch each row, ending with P13, W&T.

Shaping the Bottom of the Heel

NOTE: *To make the bottom of the heel, you will pick up a wrapped stitch at the end of each row and then turn the work. Remember to knit the wrapping and the stitch together. Slip all stitches purlwise.*

ROW 1: K14.

ROW 2: Slip 1, P14.

ROW 3: Slip 1, K15.

Continue in stockinette stitch, working 1 more stitch each row, beginning a new star as follows on row 25.

ROW 24: Slip 1, P36.

ROW 25: Slip 1, K17, P1, K19.

ROW 26: Slip 1, P38.

ROW 27: Slip 1, K18, P1, K20.

ROW 28: Slip 1, P18, K1, P1, K1, P19.

ROW 29: Slip 1, K19, P1, K19. Slip next stitch and replace beginning of round marker.

All the stitches should now be live. Do not turn the work, but begin knitting in the round again.

Knitting the Foot

ROUNDS 1–32: Follow Star 1 chart on page 84 for the stitch pattern, beginning with line 7 and working from right to left. The pattern is repeated three times around the stocking. Work lines 7–22 twice.

ROUNDS 33–47: Follow Star 3 chart on page 85 for the stitch pattern, beginning with line 1 at the bottom of the chart and working from right to left. The pattern is repeated three times around the stocking. Work chart once..

Shaping the Toe

NOTE: *When stitches become too tight for the circular needle, switch to double-pointed needles. Divide stitches evenly among three needles.*

ROUND 1: Knit to the end of the round.

ROUND 2: *K1, ssk, K8, K2tog, repeat from * to the end of the round.
You now have 66 stitches.

ROUNDS 3–6: Knit to the end of each round.

ROUND 7: *K1, ssk, K6, K2tog; repeat from * to the end of the round.
You now have 54 stitches.

ROUNDS 8–10: Knit to the end of each round.

ROUND 11: *K1, ssk, K4, K2tog; repeat from * to the end of the round.
You now have 42 stitches.

ROUNDS 12 AND 13: Knit to the end of each round.

ROUND 14: *K1, ssk, K2, K2tog; repeat from * to the end of the round.
You now have 30 stitches.

ROUND 15: Knit to the end of the round.

ROUND 16: *K1, ssk, K2tog; repeat from * to the end of the round.
You now have 18 stitches.

ROUND 17: *Slip 1, K2tog, psso; repeat from * to the end of the round.
You now have 6 stitches.

Cut yarn, thread it through a yarn needle and draw it through the remaining stitches, and pull snugly.

Making the Loop

With a double-pointed needle and MC, cast on 3 stitches, leaving an 8" tail.

Make a 6" I-cord, following the instructions for We've Got Hang-Ups on page 77.

Cut yarn, thread it through a yarn needle and draw it through the remaining stitches, and pull snugly.

Finishing

Double the I-cord to make a loop, and use the tails to sew the cord to the top of the stocking at the center back.

Weave in all loose ends on the wrong side of work.

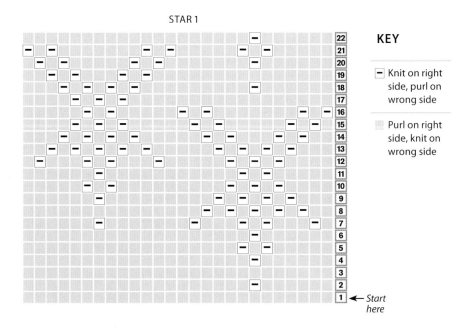

STAR 1

KEY

▭ Knit on right side, purl on wrong side

▭ Purl on right side, knit on wrong side

← Start here

Note: *It is customary in knitting books for charts to be followed from bottom to top, and, when knitting circularly, from right to left. Although this results in some charts apparently being presented upside down, the designs will be right side up when the stocking is completed.*

STAR 2

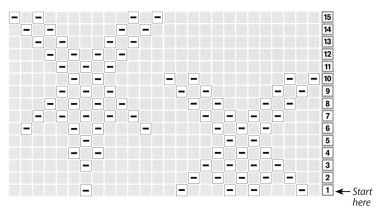

← *Start here*

STAR 3

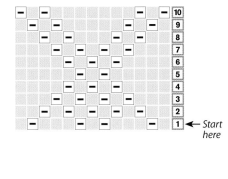

← *Start here*

Snazzy Argyles

DESIGNED BY LINDA DANIELS

Christmas stockings and argyle socks are both epitomes of tradition. With this two-color design you carry both colors as you work around the stocking — no bobbins to worry about! Once you've made one or two, you'll want to try other color combinations, as well.

FINISHED MEASUREMENTS

❋ 6¾" wide x 20" long

YARN

Brown Sheep Lamb's Pride, 85% wool/15% mohair, worsted weight, 4 oz (113 g)/190 yd (173 m) skeins

MC	Blue Flannel (M-82), 2 skeins	
CC	Red Baron (M-81), 1 skein	

NEEDLES

❋ One US 6 (4 mm) circular needle, 16" long, *or size you need to obtain correct gauge*

❋ One set of US 6 (4 mm) 10" double-pointed needles *or size you need to obtain correct gauge*

GAUGE

❋ 22 stitches = 4" on US 6 (4 mm) needles in stockinette stitch

OTHER SUPPLIES

❋ Stitch markers, crochet hook, yarn needle

ABBREVIATIONS

CC	contrasting color		MC	main color
K	knit		P	purl
K2tog	knit 2 stitches together		P2tog	purl 2 stitches together
M1	make 1 stitch		ssk	slip, slip, knit the 2 slipped stitches together

Knitting the Cuff

SETUP: With circular needle and MC, cast on 62 stitches. Join into a round, being careful not to twist the stitches. (See Getting Around, page 16, for information about knitting in the round.) Place a stitch marker to mark the beginning of the round.

ROUNDS 1–7: Knit to the end of each round.

ROUND 8: P1, *M1, P6; repeat from * nine more times; P1. (See pages 15 and 16 for how to M1.) When the project is completed, you will turn the hem under at the top of the stocking along this round of purl stitching.

You now have 72 stitches.

ROUND 9: Purl to the end of the round.

Using MC and CC, work Argyle chart (page 92), starting with line 1 at the bottom of the chart and working from right to left. The pattern repeats three times around the stocking. Work lines 1–24 twice, and then work lines 1–12 once. The leg should measure about 11".

Making the Heel Flap

SETUP: Cut the CC yarn. Using MC and a double-pointed needle, K36 for the heel flap. Leave remaining 36 stitches on the circular needle to work later for the foot. In this section, you will be working back and forth in rows, turning at the end of each row.

ROW 1 (WRONG SIDE): Slip 1, purl to the end of the row.

ROW 2 (RIGHT SIDE): *Slip 1, K1; repeat from * to the end of the row.

NEXT ROWS: Repeat rows 1 and 2 until heel flap measures 3", ending with a purl row.

Turning the Heel

ROW 1: K22, K2tog, K1, turn.

ROW 2: Slip 1, P9, P2tog, P1, turn.

ROW 3: Slip 1, K10, K2tog, K1, turn.

ROW 4: Slip 1, P11, P2tog, P1, turn.

ROW 5: Slip 1, K12, K2tog, K1, turn.

ROW 6: Slip 1, P13, P2tog, P1, turn.

ROW 7: Slip 1, K14, K2tog, K1, turn.

ROW 8: Slip 1, P15, P2tog, P1, turn.

ROW 9: Slip 1, K16, K2tog, K1, turn.

ROW 10: Slip 1, P17, P2tog, P1, turn.

ROW 11: Slip 1, K18, K2tog, K1, turn.

ROW 12: Slip 1, P19, P2tog, P1, turn.

ROW 13: Slip 1, K20, K2tog, K1, turn.

ROW 14: Slip 1, P20, P2tog, turn.

You now have 22 stitches.

Knitting the Gusset

NOTE: *For information about how to pick up along the heel, see Picking Up Stitches on page 92.*

SETUP: Using MC, CC, and the circular needle, K22 across heel flap, again working the argyle pattern. Start with stitch 8 on Argyle chart, line 13, work to stitch 24, then work stitches 1–5.

Pick up and knit 13 stitches along the left-hand side of the heel flap, working the first 7 stitches as stitches 6–12 of the Argyle chart, then work the last 6 stitches in MC. Place a stitch marker.

K36 from circular needle, following Argyle chart line 13, stitches 13–24, then stitches 1–24. Place a stitch marker.

Pick up and knit 13 stitches along the right-hand side of the heel flap in this manner: work the first 6 stitches in MC, place a stitch marker for the beginning round. Start new round here with the first stitch of Argyle chart line 14 and continue in pattern.

You now have 84 stitches.

From here on, follow the Argyle chart, except for the two MC blocks at the sides of the foot. You will make the decreases in these MC stitches.

ROUND 1: Knit in pattern to the last 3 stitches before the first marker, K2tog, K1, slip marker, knit to next marker, slip marker, K1, ssk, knit to end of round.

You now have 82 stitches.

ROUND 2: Knit even to the end of the round.

ROUNDS 3–12: Repeat rounds 1 and 2, keeping the stitches in the decrease areas before the first marker and after the second marker in MC.

After row 12, *you now have* 72 stitches, and the chart pattern fits evenly all around (three complete repeats). Remove markers.

Knitting the Foot

Continue following Argyle chart until foot measures about 7" from the heel flap, ending with chart line 1.

Shaping the Toe

SETUP: Cut the yarn and slip the stitches to double-pointed needles as follows:

- ❋ Slip 11 stitches to an empty needle.
- ❋ Slip 18 stitches to another empty needle.
- ❋ Slip 36 stitches to another empty needle.
- ❋ Slip 7 stitches to the needle that holds the first 11 stitches.

The stitches are arranged as follows:

> **Needle 1:** 18 stitches
> **Needle 2:** 36 stitches
> **Needle 3:** 18 stitches

ROUND 1: Using MC and beginning with Needle 1, knit to the end of the round.

ROUND 2:

> **Needle 1:** Knit to the last 3 stitches, K2tog, K1.
> **Needle 2:** K1, ssk, knit to the last 3 stitches, K2tog, K1.
> **Needle 3:** K1, ssk, knit to the end of the round.

You now have 68 stitches arranged as follows:

> **Needle 1:** 17 stitches
>
> **Needle 2:** 34 stitches
>
> **Needle 3:** 17 stitches

ROUNDS 3–14: Repeat round 2 until you have 20 stitches arranged as follows:

> **Needle 1:** 5 stitches
>
> **Needle 2:** 10 stitches
>
> **Needle 3:** 5 stitches

Knit the stitches from Needle 1 onto Needle 3.

Graft the front and back together using Kitchener stitch. (For instructions, see Kitchener Stitch on page 93.)

Finishing

Cut the yarn and weave in all loose ends.

Fold hem along the purl row, and sew it to inside of stocking with an overcast stitch. Block the stocking (see Stocking Blocking, page 21). Make a Twisted Bundle hanger (see below).

TWISTED BUNDLES

Take 12 strands of yarn 12" long and tie them together at one end with an overhand knot. (Use six strands of each color.) Have someone hold the knot or anchor it to a stationary object. Take six strands in each hand (use six of the same color or three of each, for different effects), and twist each group very tightly in the same direction. Bring the two groups together and tie another overhand knot at the opposite end, allowing the two groups to twist around each other, forming a twisted cord. Fold the cord again, and sew each end to the inside of the hem at the back of the stocking. (See photo on page 77.)

ARGYLE

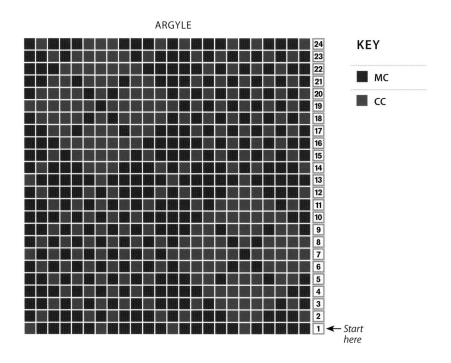

24
23
22
21
20
19
18
17
16
15
14
13
12
11
10
9
8
7
6
5
4
3
2
1 ← *Start here*

KEY

■ MC

■ CC

PICKING UP STITCHES

To pick up stitches, slide a crochet hook through the space just below the bound-off edge. Pull the yarn through and place a newly created stitch on the left-hand needle.

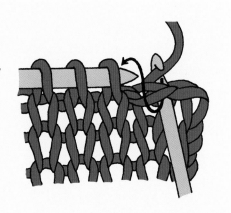

KITCHENER STITCH

1. Hold two fabric layers together with wrong sides facing each other. Thread the yarn through a yarn needle, and insert the needle through the first stitch of front needle as if to knit. Drawing the yarn through the stitch, slip the stitch off the needle.

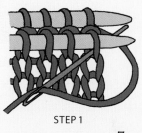

STEP 1

2. Insert the yarn needle through the second stitch of the front needle as if to purl; draw yarn through, but leave the stitch on the needle.

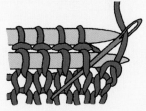

STEP 2

3. Insert the yarn needle through the first stitch of the back needle as if to purl; draw the yarn through and slip the stitch off.

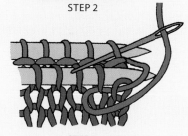

STEP 3

4. Insert the yarn needle through the second stitch of the back needle as if to knit; draw the yarn through, but leave the stitch on the needle.

Repeat steps 1–4 until you have worked all stitches and none remain on needles.

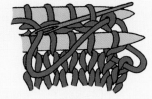

STEP 4

Gifted Stocking

DESIGNED BY LINDA DANIELS

Gifts are the theme of this whimsical stocking. Appliqués of beribboned boxes provide small pockets for tucking in tiny extras on the outside, while the roomy stocking can be stuffed with more treats. The pockets and zigzag cuff are all knit separately, so the plain-knit stocking knits up quickly.

FINISHED MEASUREMENTS

❊ 7¼" wide x 18½" long

YARN

Classic Elite Minnow Merino, 100% superwash Merino, worsted weight, 1.75 oz (50 g)/77 yd (70 m) skeins

❊ **MC** Rogue (4758), 2 skeins

❊ **CC** Elderberry (4727), 1 skein

❊ **Gifts** Here's an opportunity to use your stash! For the stocking shown, we used Brown Sheep Lamb's Pride (85% wool/15% mohair) in white and Amethyst (M-62), and the Classic Elite Minnow Merino (CC in the pattern) in Elderberry held together with a strand of Anchor Artiste Metallic in Gold (300).

NEEDLES

❊ One US 8 (5 mm) circular needle, 16" long, *or size you need to obtain correct gauge*

❊ One set of US 8 (5 mm) double-pointed needles *or size you need to obtain correct gauge*

GAUGE

❊ 16 stitches = 4" on US 8 (5 mm) needles in stockinette stitch

OTHER SUPPLIES

❊ Stitch markers (one in a unique color), H/8 (5 mm) crochet hook, yarn needle

ABBREVIATIONS

CC	contrasting color	MC	main color
ch	chain (crochet)	P	purl
K	knit	P2tog	purl 2 stitches together
K2tog	knit 2 stitches together	ssk	slip, slip, knit the 2 slipped stitches together
M1	make 1 stitch		

Knitting the Cuff

SETUP: Using CC and double-pointed needles, cast on 9 stitches.

ROW 1: K7, M1, K2.

You now have 10 stitches. (See pages 15 and 16 for how to M1.)

ROWS 2, 4, 6, 8, AND 10: Knit to the end of each row.

ROW 3: K8, M1, K2.

You now have 11 stitches.

ROW 5: K9, M1, K2.

You now have 12 stitches.

ROW 7: K10, M1, K2.

You now have 13 stitches.

ROW 9: K11, M1, K2.

You now have 14 stitches.

ROW 11: K12, M1, K2.

You now have 15 stitches.

ROWS 12–15: Knit to the end of each row.

ROW 16: Bind off 6 stitches. Knit to the end of the row.

You now have 9 stitches.

NEXT ROWS: Repeat rows 1–16 until the cuff measures 14", ending with row 16.

Bind off all stitches, and sew the cast-on and bound-off edges together to form a ring. You will sew this cuff onto the stocking after it is completed.

Knitting the Leg

SETUP: Using MC and the circular needle, cast on 58 stitches. Place a stitch marker on the needle and join into a round, taking care not to twist the stitches. (See Getting Around, page 16, for information about knitting in the round.)

Knit every round (stockinette stitch) until the leg measures 10". Cut MC.

Making the Heel Flap

SETUP: Using CC and one double-pointed needle, knit across the first 29 stitches. Leave the remaining stitches on the circular needle.

NOTE: *You will be working back and forth in rows on two double-pointed needles in this section.*

ROW 1 (WRONG SIDE): Purl to the end of the row. Turn.

ROW 2 (RIGHT SIDE): Knit to the end of the row. Turn.

NEXT ROWS: Repeat rows 1 and 2 until the heel flap measures 2½", ending with a purl (wrong-side) row.

Turning the Heel

ROW 1 (RIGHT SIDE): K19, ssk, K1. Turn. *(7 stitches remain unworked.)*

ROW 2 (WRONG SIDE): Slip 1, P10, P2tog, P1. Turn. *(7 stitches remain unworked.)*

ROW 3: Slip 1, K11, ssk, K1. Turn.

ROW 4: Slip 1, P12, P2tog, P1. Turn.

ROW 5: Slip 1, K13, ssk, K1. Turn.

ROW 6: Slip 1, P14, P2tog, P1. Turn.

ROW 7: Slip 1, K15, ssk, K1. Turn.

ROW 8: Slip 1, P16, P2tog, P1. Turn.

ROW 9: Slip 1, K17, ssk. Turn.

ROW 10: P18, P2tog. Turn. All the stitches have been worked, and *you now have* 19 stitches remaining. Cut CC.

Knitting the Gusset and Foot

NOTE: *For information about how to pick up along the heel, see Picking Up Stitches, page 92.*

SETUP:

* Using MC and the circular needle, knit the 19 stitches just worked (heel flap), pick up and knit 11 stitches along the left-hand side of the heel flap, place marker.

✳ Knit the 29 stitches that you left on the circular needle, place a second stitch marker.

✳ Pick up and knit 11 stitches along the right-hand side of the heel flap.

✳ K9, place a third stitch marker in a unique color to indicate the beginning of the round (at the center bottom of the foot). You now have 70 stitches.

ROUND 1: Knit to 3 stitches before the first stitch marker, K2tog, K1, slip the stitch marker, knit to the next stitch marker, slip the stitch marker, K1, ssk, knit to the end of the round.

You now have 68 stitches.

ROUND 2: Knit to the end of the round.

ROUNDS 3–12: Repeat rounds 1 and 2. After round 12, *you now have* 58 stitches.

NEXT ROUNDS: Knit even in stockinette stitch until the foot measures 6" from the bottom of the heel flap (where you began working in rounds again). Cut MC.

Shaping the Toe

SETUP: Using CC, knit stitches from the circular needle onto double-pointed needles, as follows:

> **Needle 1:** K15.
>
> **Needle 2:** K29.
>
> **Needle 3:** K14.

ROUND 1:

> **Needle 1:** Knit to the last 3 stitches, K2tog, K1. You now have 14 stitches on this needle.
>
> **Needle 2:** K1, ssk, knit to the last 3 stitches, K2tog, K1. You now have 27 stitches on this needle.
>
> **Needle 3:** K1, ssk, knit to the end of the round. You now have 13 stitches on this needle.

ROUNDS 2–11: Repeat round 1.

You now have 14 stitches.

Knit the 4 stitches from Needle 3 onto Needle 1. Graft the front and back together using Kitchener stitch. (See Kitchener Stitch on page 93.)

Knitting the Presents

SETUP: Using the white yarn and double-pointed needles, cast on 7 stitches. Work in stockinette stitch (knit on the right side, purl on the wrong side) back and forth in rows, turning at the end of each row, until the piece measures 3". Bind off all stitches.

With the Elderberry and Gold metallic yarns held together and two double-pointed needles, cast on 16 stitches. Work back and forth in stockinette stitch until the piece measures 2". Bind off all stitches.

With the Amethyst yarn and two double-pointed needles, cast on 12 stitches. Work back and forth in stockinette stitch until the piece measures 2". Bind off all stitches.

Finishing

Hiding your stitches in the yarn, sew the presents to one side of stocking leg as shown in the photo on page 95, placing the white pocket first, then the Elderberry, and finally the Amethyst. Leave the tops open to create pockets.

THE TIES: For the white package, cast on 2 stitches and work I-cord for 3" (see We've Got Hang-Ups, page 77, for instructions). Do not fasten off. Use the crochet hook to pull one of the stitches through the other, then ch 10, * slip stitch into the first chain stitch, ch 10; repeat from * three more times; slip stitch into the first chain stitch and fasten off. You have formed four "bow" loops. Repeat for the other two packages, making the tie for the Amethyst package 2" long, and making two ties for the mixed-yarn package, one measuring the width and the other measuring the length of the package; work the bow separately for this package. Tack all the bows and ties to the packages, taking care not to sew the pockets closed.

With the yarn needle, use an overhand stitch to sew the straight edge of the cuff to the top of the stocking, with the right side of the cuff facing the wrong side of the stocking. Turn the cuff to the right side of the stocking and tack it in place. Weave in all the loose ends.

THE HANGER: Using CC and a double-pointed needle, pick up 3 stitches at the top of the cuff at the back of the stocking. Work a 5" I-cord. Cut the yarn and pull it through all the stitches. Use the end to sew the hanger to the stocking where the I-cord begins. (See page 77.)

Victorian Flowers

DESIGNED BY GWEN STEEGE

If you're looking for something a bit more feminine, we hope you'll enjoy making this romantic stocking. The ribbed effect is created by slipping every other stitch on alternate rounds, not only giving the stocking an interesting texture, but also making it surprisingly quick and easy to knit. After the stocking is knitted, decorate it with simple embroidery stitches. On page 105, you'll find illustrations of how to do the feather and laced running stitches shown here, or use your own favorite designs. Crocheted flowers add the final touch.

FINISHED MEASUREMENTS

❀ 5" wide x 17" long

YARN

Tahki Yarns Cotton Classic, 100% mercerized cotton, 1.75 oz (50 g)/108 yd (100 m) skeins
MC   Linen White (#3003), 2 skeins
CC   Dark Celery (#3752), 1 skein

ABBREVIATIONS

ch	chain (crochet)
CC	contrasting color
K	knit
K2tog	knit 2 stitches together
MC	main color
P	purl
P2tog	purl 2 stitches together
sc	single crochet
ssk	slip, slip, knit the 2 slipped stitches together

NEEDLES

❀ One set of US 6 (4 mm) double-pointed needles *or size you need to obtain correct gauge*

GAUGE

❀ 26 stitches = 4" on US 6 (4 mm) needles in pattern stitch

OTHER SUPPLIES

❀ Stitch holder, I-9 (5.5 mm) crochet hook, yarn needle, embroidery floss or yarn (optional)

Knitting the Cuff

SETUP: Using MC, cast on 60 stitches. Distribute stitches evenly among three needles and join into a round. (For information about working in the round with double-pointed needles, see Getting Around, page 16.)

ROUNDS 1 AND 2: With MC, knit to the end of the round.

ROUND 3: Change to CC, and knit to the end of the round.

ROUND 4: Purl to the end of the round.

ROUND 5: Change to MC, and knit to the end of the round.

ROUNDS 6–14: Repeat rounds 3–5.

Knitting the Leg

ROUND 1: With MC, knit to the end of the round.

ROUND 2: *K1, slip 1 with the needle in back of the stitch; repeat from * to the end of the round.

NEXT ROUNDS: Repeat rounds 1 and 2 until work measures 11" from cast-on edge, ending with round 2. Cut the yarn, leaving a 3" tail to work in later.

Making the Heel Flap

SETUP: Place the first 15 stitches on one needle. Place the next 30 stitches on a stitch holder. Place the remaining 15 stitches on the needle with the first 15 stitches.

NOTE: *You will be working back and forth in rows in garter stitch (knitting every row) in this section.*

ROW 1 (RIGHT SIDE): With MC, knit to the end of the needle.

ROW 2 (WRONG SIDE): Slip 1, knit to the end of the needle.

ROW 3: Change to CC. Slip 1, knit to the end of the needle.

ROW 4: Slip 1, knit to the end of the needle.

ROW 5: Change to MC. Slip 1, knit to the end of the needle.

ROW 6: Slip 1, knit to the end of the needle.

ROW 7: Change to CC. Slip 1, knit to the end of the needle.

ROW 8: Slip 1, knit to the end of the needle.

NEXT ROWS: Repeat rows 5–8 until heel flap measures 2½", ending with row 8.

Turning the Heel

ROW 1: With CC, K19, ssk, K1, turn. (*8 stitches remain unworked on needle.*)

ROW 2: Slip 1, P9, P2tog, P1, turn. (*8 stitches remain unworked.*)

ROW 3: Slip 1, knit until 1 stitch remains before the gap formed in the previous row, ssk, K1, turn.

ROW 4: Slip 1, purl until 1 stitch remains before the gap formed in the previous row, P2tog, P1, turn.

NEXT ROWS: Repeat rows 3 and 4 until all stitches have been worked, ending with a purl row.

You now have 20 stitches.

NEXT ROW: Knit to the end of the row. Cut the yarn, leaving a tail to work in later.

Knitting the Gusset

SETUP: Place 10 heel stitches on Needle 1 and the remaining 10 stitches on Needle 3. Place 30 stitches from the stitch holder (instep stitches) on Needle 2.

PICKUP ROUND:

Needle 1: Join MC at the beginning of Needle 1. Knit to the end of the needle. Pick up and knit 16 stitches along the left-hand side of the heel flap. (See Picking Up Stitches, page 92.)

Needle 2: Knit to the end of the needle.

Needle 3: Using an empty needle, pick up and knit 16 stitches along the right-hand side of the heel flap, knit to the end of the needle, K10 from the bottom of the heel.

You now have on

Needle 1: 26 stitches

Needle 2: 30 stitches

Needle 3: 26 stitches

ROUND 1: Knit to the end of the round.

ROUND 2:

    Needle 1: Knit to the last 3 stitches, K2tog, K1.

    Needle 2: Knit to the end of the needle.

    Needle 3: K1, ssk, knit to the end of the needle.

ROUND 3: *K1, slip 1 with the needle in back of the stitch; repeat from * to the end of the round.

NEXT ROUNDS: Repeat rounds 2 and 3 until Needles 1 and 3 have 15 stitches each (60 stitches in total), ending with round 2.

Knitting the Foot

ROUND 1: *K1, slip 1 with the needle in the back of the stitch; repeat from * to the end of the round.

ROUND 2: Knit to the end of the round.

NEXT ROUNDS: Repeat rounds 1 and 2 until the foot measures 4½" along the center bottom from the end of the heel (the end of CC).

Shaping the Toe

ROUND 1: Change to CC. Knit to the end of the round.

ROUND 2: With CC, purl to the end of the round.

ROUND 3: Change to MC. *K3, K2tog; repeat from * to the end of the round. *You now have* 48 stitches.

ROUNDS 4 AND 5: Change to CC, and repeat rounds 1 and 2.

ROUND 6: Change to MC. *K2, K2tog; repeat from * to the end of the round. *You now have* 36 stitches.

ROUNDS 7 AND 8: Change to CC, and repeat rounds 1 and 2.

ROUND 9: Change to MC. *K1, K2tog; repeat from * to the end of the round. *You now have* 24 stitches.

ROUNDS 10 AND 11: Change to CC, and repeat rounds 1 and 2.

ROUND 12: Change to MC. *K2tog; repeat from * to the end of the round.
You now have 12 stitches.

Cut the yarn, leaving a 10" tail. Draw yarn through the remaining stitches. Fasten
off on the inside.

Finishing

THE CROCHETED EDGE: With CC, sc along the top edge of the stocking. Then, *ch 5,
skip 3, slip into next single chain; repeat from * around.

THE HANGER: With CC, chain for 3". Form a loop by slipping into first stitch. Sc
in the loop, working around the loop to cover it completely. (Push the single
chains back tightly as you work, in order to keep the loop flat.) Fasten off. (See
also page 77.)

EMBROIDERY: With CC, use laced running stitch and feather stitch (see below) to
decorate as shown on page 101.

THE CROCHETED FLOWERS: With CC, ch 5; join into a loop. Sc 15 in the loop. *Ch 5,
skip 2, slip into next sc; repeat from * to the end of the round.

You now have made five "petals." Fasten off. Make four more flowers in the same
manner, and sew them in place (see photo, page 101).

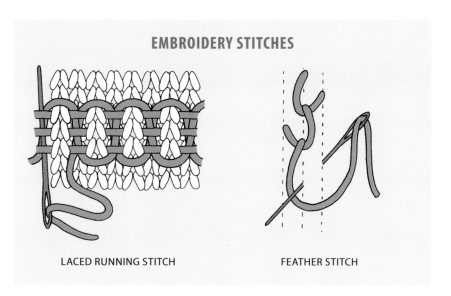

EMBROIDERY STITCHES

LACED RUNNING STITCH   FEATHER STITCH

Mini Socks

DESIGNED BY NANCY LINDBERG

This miniature sock knits up quickly in heavyweight yarn. Like its big brother, the Mix-and-Match Stockings on page 60, it features an "afterthought heel." You'll knit the stocking straight down to the toe and then add the heel afterward, when you're done. These stockings make great ornaments, or tuck a small gift inside for a special friend.

FINISHED MEASUREMENTS

❋ 3" wide x 7" long

YARN

Brown Sheep Lamb's Pride, 85% wool/15% mohair, worsted weight, 4 oz (113 g)/190 yd (173 m) skeins

MC	White Frost (M11)/Amethyst (M62), 13 yds
CC A	Violet Fields (M161)/Old Sage (M69), 12 yds
CC B	Aztec Turquoise (M78)/Sandy Heather (M01), 15 yds

NEEDLES

❋ One set of US 8 (5 mm) double-pointed needles *or size you need to obtain correct gauge*

GAUGE

❋ 20 stitches = 4" on US 8 (5 mm) needles in stockinette stitch

OTHER SUPPLIES

❋ Small quantity of scrap yarn in similar weight, yarn needle

ABBREVIATIONS

CC	contrasting color	MC	main color
K	knit	P	purl
K2tog	knit 2 stitches together	ssk	slip, slip, knit the 2 slipped stitches together

Knitting the Cuff

SETUP: Using MC and double-pointed needles, cast on 30 stitches, leaving a tail of yarn 1 yd (1 m) long. Distribute the stitches evenly among three needles (10 stitches per needle), and join into a round, taking care not to twist the stitches. For information about knitting in the round, see Getting Around on page 16.

ROUNDS 1–4: Work in K1, P1 ribbing.

Knitting the Leg

ROUNDS 1–20: Using MC, CC A, and CC B, knit each round, following lines 1–20 on the Mini-Sock chart on page 110 for the color pattern. Begin where indicated on line 1 at the bottom of the chart and work from right to left. Repeat each pattern three times in each round. For more information about knitting color patterns, see The Joy of Color, page 19. Cut MC after working line 1, but do not cut CC A between rounds. Work round 11 with only CC B; add MC later in Duplicate Stitch (see page 111).

Marking for the Heel

SETUP: When you have completed line 20 of the chart, cut CC A and B. Slide the last 7 stitches just worked to an empty needle (now Needle 3). Slide the remaining 3 stitches onto Needle 2.

Join scrap yarn at the beginning of Needle 3, and knit the 7 stitches onto it.

Continuing with the scrap yarn, knit the first 8 stitches on Needle 1, then slide the remaining 2 stitches onto Needle 2. Cut the scrap yarn.

The stitches are now distributed as follows:

  Needle 1: 8 stitches
  Needle 2: 15 stitches
  Needle 3: 7 stitches

Knitting the Foot

Join CC A at the beginning of Needle 2, which will now be at the start of each round.

ROUNDS 1–11: Using CC A, continue to work the Mini-Sock chart, picking it up again at line 21. Knit to the end of each round.

After round 11, *you now have* completed all 31 lines of the chart. Cut CC A and B.

Shaping the Toe

ROUND 1: Using MC, knit to the end of the round.

ROUND 2 (DECREASE ROUND):

Needle 2: Ssk, knit to the last 2 stitches, K2tog.
You now have 13 stitches on the needle.

Needle 3: Ssk, knit to the end of the needle.
You now have 6 stitches on the needle.

Needle 1: Knit to the last 2 stitches, K2tog.
You now have 7 stitches on the needle.

ROUNDS 3–8: Repeat rounds 1 and 2.

After round 8, *you now have* 14 stitches.

Place the stitches from Needles 1 and 3 on the same needle, and then graft the toe using Kitchener Stitch (page 93).

Making the Afterthought Heel

SETUP: Carefully pull out the scrap yarn, picking up the live stitches from the rows above and below and placing them on two needles. *You now have* 15 stitches on each needle. Redistribute them as follows:

- ✻ Needle 2 has 15 stitches from the upper row. (This needle will be at the start of round, as for the foot.)
- ✻ Needle 3 has 7 stitches from the lower row.
- ✻ Needle 1 has 8 stitches from the lower row.

Join MC at the beginning of Needle 2. Follow instructions for rounds 1–8 under Shaping the Toe, above.

Making the Loop

At the top of the sock, using the tail from the cast on, pick up and knit 2 stitches. (See Picking Up Stitches on page 92.)

Knit a 2½" I-cord, following the instructions in We've Got Hang-Ups on page 77.

Tie off the I-cord and tack the other end to the sock using the yarn needle.

Finishing

With MC and Duplicate Stitch, add the holly berries as shown on the Mini-Sock chart. (See Duplicate Stitch, right.)

Cut the yarn and weave in all loose ends on the wrong side of your work.

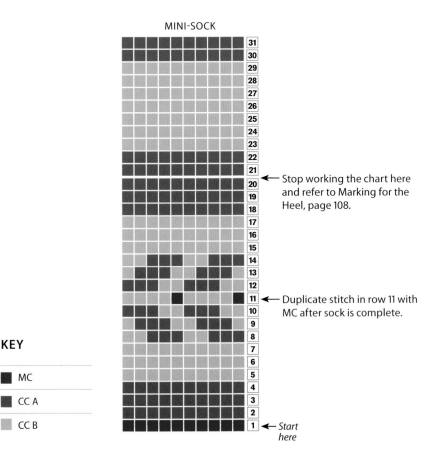

MINI-SOCK

← Stop working the chart here and refer to Marking for the Heel, page 108.

← Duplicate stitch in row 11 with MC after sock is complete.

KEY

- ■ MC
- ■ CC A
- □ CC B

← Start here

DUPLICATE STITCH

STEP 1: Bring the yarn needle out from the center of the stitch below the stitch to be covered.

STEP 2: Insert the needle through both sides of the V of the stitch above the one to be covered and pull the yarn through, thus covering half the stitch.

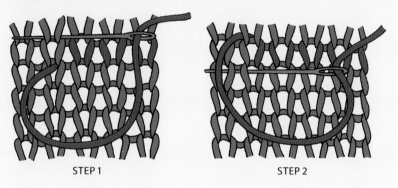

STEP 1   STEP 2

STEP 3: Insert the needle again into the original hole (that is, the center of the stitch below the stitch being covered).

Work from the bottom to the top to cover vertical stitches and from right to left and then left to right to cover horizontal stitches.

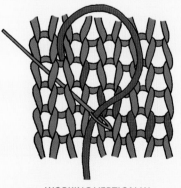 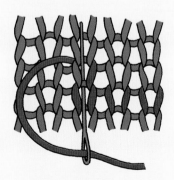

WORKING VERTICALLY   WORKING HORIZONTALLY

A Heart, a Star, and a Tree

DESIGNED BY EVELYN A. CLARK

These heart, tree, and star ornaments are all knitted in garter stitch outlined with eyelets, then felted. Leave them plain, or embellish them with buttons, beads, or ribbons. Be sure to use a yarn that will felt well (see Yarns for Felting, page 7, for advice). We used worsted-weight yarn, but you can try different weight yarns to make smaller or larger items.

FINISHED MEASUREMENTS *(after felting)*

※ **Heart:** 4" wide
※ **Tree:** 5" wide x 5" tall
※ **Star:** 4" wide

YARN

Cascade 220, 100% Peruvian Highland wool, worsted weight, 3½ oz (100 g)/220 yd (200 m) skeins
 Heart: Hot Pink (9469), 15 yds
 Tree: Christmas Green Heather (9490), 15 yds
 Star: Natural (4528), 16 yds

NEEDLES

※ **Heart and Tree:** One pair of US 11 (8 mm) straight needles *or size you need to obtain correct gauge*
※ **Star:** One set of US 11 (8 mm) double-pointed needles *or size you need to obtain correct gauge*

GAUGE

※ 12 stitches = 4" on US 11 (8 mm) needles in garter stitch

OTHER SUPPLIES

※ Yarn needle, safety pin, beads and/ or buttons, ¼" wide ribbon or cord, matching sewing thread and needle

ABBREVIATIONS

K	knit	ssk	slip, slip, knit the 2 slipped stitches together
K2tog	knit 2 stitches together		
psso	pass slipped stitch over	yo	yarn over

THE HEART

SETUP: With straight needles, cast on 5 stitches.

ROW 1: *K1, increase 1 by knitting into the front and back of the next stitch; repeat from * one more time, K1.

You now have 7 stitches.

ALL EVEN-NUMBERED ROWS: Knit to the end of each row.

NOTE: *Row 3 begins the eyelet outline. When working even-numbered rows, knit yo stitches from the previous row.*

ROW 3: K1, yo, K2tog, yo, K1, yo, ssk, yo, K1. *You now have 9 stitches.*

ROW 5: K1, yo, K7, yo, K1. *You now have 11 stitches.*

ROW 7: K1, yo, K9, yo, K1. *You now have 13 stitches.*

ROW 9: K1, yo, ssk, K9, yo, K1. *You now have 14 stitches.*

ROW 11: K1, yo, ssk, K10, yo, K1. *You now have 15 stitches.*

ROWS 13 AND 15: Ssk, yo, ssk, K10, yo, K1. *You still have 15 stitches.*

ROWS 17 AND 19: K1, yo, K10, K2tog, yo, K2tog. *You still have 15 stitches.*

ROW 21: K1, yo, ssk, K8, K2tog, yo, K2tog. *You now have 14 stitches.*

ROW 23: K1, yo, ssk, K7, K2tog, yo, K2tog. *You now have 13 stitches.*

ROW 25: Ssk, yo, ssk, K5, K2tog, yo, K2tog. *You now have 11 stitches.*

ROW 27: Ssk, yo, ssk, yo, slip 1 knitwise, K2tog, psso, yo, K2tog, yo, K2tog. *You now have 9 stitches.*

ROW 29: Ssk twice, K1, K2tog twice. *You now have 5 stitches.*

Bind off all stitches, cut the yarn, and weave in all loose ends.

THE TREE

With straight needles, cast on 2 stitches.

ALL ODD-NUMBERED ROWS THROUGH ROW 23: Knit to end of each row.

ROW 2: K1, yo, K1. *You now have 3 stitches.*

ROW 4: K1, (yo, K1) twice. *You now have* 5 stitches.

ROW 6: K1, yo, K2tog, (yo, K1) twice. *You now have* 7 stitches.

ROW 8: K1, yo, K5, yo, K1. *You now have* 9 stitches.

ROW 10: K1, (yo, K2tog) three times, (yo, K1) twice. *You now have* 11 stitches.

ROW 12: K1, yo, K9, yo, K1. *You now have* 13 stitches.

ROW 14: K1, (yo, K2tog) five times, (yo, K1) twice. *You now have* 15 stitches.

ROW 16: K1, yo, K13, yo, K1. *You now have* 17 stitches.

ROW 18: K1, (yo, K2tog) seven times, (yo, K1) twice. *You now have* 19 stitches.

ROW 20: K1, yo, K17, yo, K1. *You now have* 21 stitches.

ROW 22: K1, (yo, K2tog) nine times, (yo, K1) twice. *You now have* 23 stitches.

ROW 24: Bind off 9 stitches, knit to the end of the row. *You now have* 14 stitches.

ROW 25: Bind off 9 stitches, knit to the end of the row. *You now have* 5 stitches.

ROWS 26–30: Knit to the end of each row.

Bind off all stitches, cut the yarn, and weave in all loose ends.

THE STAR

Making the Points

NOTE: *The points of the star are knitted back and forth in rows first, then joined and worked in rounds on double-pointed needles to the center.*

SETUP: With straight needles, cast on 2 stitches.

ROWS 1, 3, AND 5: Knit to end of each row.

ROW 2: K1, yo, K1. *You now have* 3 stitches.

ROW 4: K1, (yo, K1) twice. *You now have* 5 stitches.

❋ Cut the yarn, leaving an 8" tail. Slip the stitches onto a double-pointed needle.

❋ Repeat rows 1–5 four more times (making five points in all). Transfer each of the points to double-pointed needles, placing two points on each needle. Leave the fifth point on the current needle. Do not cut the yarn after the last point.

Knitting the Center

SETUP: Distribute the stitches so that Needle 1 has the last point knitted (5 stitches), and Needles 2 and 3 each have two points (10 stitches). Begin working in the round, being careful not to twist the stitches when you join between each needle. (For information about knitting in the round, see Getting Around, page 16.) Place a locking stitch marker or a safety pin on the first stitch on Needle 1 to mark the beginning of the round. *You now have* 25 stitches.

ROUND 1:

Needle 1: K1, yo, K3, yo, K1. You now have 7 stitches on this needle.

Needle 2: (K1, yo, K3, yo, K1) twice. You now have 14 stitches on this needle.

Needle 3: (K1, yo, K3, yo, K1) twice. You now have 14 stitches on this needle and 35 stitches altogether.

ROUNDS 2, 4, 6, 8, AND 10: Purl to the end of each round.

ROUNDS 3 AND 5: Knit to the end of each round.

ROUND 7: *K1, ssk, K1, K2tog, K1; repeat from * to the end of the round. *You now have* 25 stitches.

ROUND 9: *Ssk, K1, K2tog; repeat from * to the end of the round. *You now have* 15 stitches.

ROUND 11: *Slip 1 knitwise, K2tog, psso; repeat from * to the end of the round. *You now have* 5 stitches.

※ Cut the yarn, leaving an 8" tail. Thread the tail on a yarn needle, and draw it through the remaining stitches and tighten.

※ Weave in all loose ends on the wrong side of the work.

KNOWING WHAT'S RIGHT

When knitting garter stitch, it's helpful to hang a safety pin on the edge of the front of the fabric to mark the beginning of right-side rows.

Finishing

Felt ornaments by hand or in a washing machine, following the advice in Felting on page 125. To speed felting, first soak the ornament in cold water for at least 20 minutes. When felting is completed, rinse and pull the ornament into shape. If fibers have felted over the eyelets, hold the ornament up to light and use a yarn needle to separate the fibers. Lay flat to dry.

Decorate ornaments as desired, using buttons or beads, ribbons, and/or embroidery. Use matching sewing thread on a sewing needle to attach beads in eyelet holes. Bury thread in the thick felted fabric, coming up with the needle at each eyelet, threading a bead in place and then working on to the next eyelet. Always work horizontally.

To make a hanger, cut 10" of narrow ribbon or cord, thread it through the top eyelet, and knot it.

Mini Felted Mitts and Socks

DESIGNED BY BEVERLY GALESKAS

These miniatures may not have room for all the goodies Santa brings, but they make festive accents on any tree. Knit them large, then felt and shrink them to ornament size. For advice on yarns, see Yarns for Felting, page 7.

MEASUREMENTS (FINISHED)

Stocking: 2¾" wide x 6" long
Mitten: 2¾" wide x 4½" long

YARN

Cascade 220, 100% Peruvian Highland wool, worsted weight, 3½ oz (100 g)/220 yd (200 m) skeins, Natural (4528), Hot Pink (9469), Christmas Green Heather (9490), Marine (8339)

Sock
| MC | 30 yds |
| CC A | 5 yds |

Mitt
| MC | 35 yds |
| CC A | 3 yds |

NEEDLES

※ One set of US 10½ (6.5 mm) double-pointed needles *or size you need to obtain correct gauge*

GAUGE

※ 12–14 stitches = 4" on US 10½ (6.5 mm) needles in stockinette stitch

OTHER SUPPLIES

※ Stitch holder, crochet hook, yarn needle, felting supplies (fine-mesh bag, jeans, washing machine, detergent; see page 125), buttons and/or 3 yds embroidery yarn and needle (optional)

ABBREVIATIONS

CC	contrasting color
K	knit
K2tog	knit 2 stitches together
M1	make 1 stitch
MC	main color
P	purl
P2tog	purl 2 stitches together
ssk	slip, slip, knit the 2 slipped stitches together

THE SOCK

Knitting the Cuff

SETUP: Cast on 22 stitches.

ROWS 1–4: Knit to the end of each row. (This is the garter-stitch cuff, which will be seamed after the stocking is completed.)

Knitting the Stocking

SETUP: Distribute the stitches evenly among three double-pointed needles. Join into a round, taking care not to twist any stitches. For information on circular knitting, see Getting Around on page 16.

ROUNDS 1–14: Using MC, knit to the end of each round.

Knitting the Heel

Join CC A without cutting the MC yarn. You will be working back and forth in rows in this and the next section.

ROW 1 (RIGHT SIDE): K12. Place remaining stitches on a stitch holder, if desired.

ROW 2: Purl to the end of the row.

ROW 3: Knit to the end of the row.

ROWS 4–7: Repeat rows 2 and 3 on the 12 stitches you are working.

Turning the Heel

ROW 1 (WRONG SIDE): P7, P2tog, P1, turn.

ROW 2: Slip 1, K3, K2tog, K1, turn.

ROW 3: Slip 1, P4, P2tog, P1, turn.

ROW 4: Slip 1, K5, K2tog, K1, turn.

ROW 5: P6, P2tog, turn.

ROW 6: K5, K2tog. Cut CC A. *You now have* 6 stitches.

Knitting the Gusset and Foot

SETUP: Beginning with the right side of the heel facing you, where MC is still attached, pick up and distribute stitches as follows (see Picking Up Stitches, page 92):

> **Needle 1:** With a new needle, pick up and knit 6 stitches along the side of the heel, then K3 from the heel.
>
> **Needle 2:** K3 from the bottom of the heel, then pick up and knit 6 stitches along the other side of the heel.
>
> **Needle 3:** K10 (instep).

You now have 28 stitches, distributed as follows:

> **Needle 1:** 9 stitches
>
> **Needle 2:** 9 stitches
>
> **Needle 3:** 10 stitches

ROUND 1: Knit to the end of the round.

ROUND 2:

> **Needle 1:** Ssk, knit to the end of the needle.
>
> **Needle 2:** Knit to the last 2 stitches on the needle, K2tog.
>
> **Needle 3:** Knit to the end of the needle.

ROUNDS 3–6: Repeat rounds 1 and 2. *You now have* 22 stitches.

ROUNDS 7–9: Knit to the end of each round. Cut MC.

Shaping the Toe

ROUND 1: Using CC A, knit to the end of the round.

ROUND 2:

> **Needle 1:** K1, K2tog, knit to the end of the needle.
>
> **Needle 2:** Knit to the last 3 stitches on the needle, ssk, K1.
>
> **Needle 3:** K2tog, knit to the last 2 stitches, ssk.

ROUNDS 3–8: Repeat rounds 1 and 2. At the end of round 8, *you now have* 6 stitches. Cut yarn.

With a yarn needle, thread the yarn through the remaining stitches and pull firmly. Fasten off. Go to Finishing (page 124).

THE MITT

Knitting the Cuff

SETUP: Using CC A, cast on 20 stitches.

ROWS 1–4: Knit to the end of each row. Cut CC A. (This is a garter-stitch cuff, which will be seamed when the mitt is completed.)

Knitting the Thumb Gusset

SETUP: Distribute the 20 stitches evenly among three double-pointed needles. Join into a round, taking care not to twist the stitches. (For advice on knitting in the round, see Getting Around on page 16.)

ROUNDS 1 AND 2: Using MC, knit to the end of each round.

ROUND 3: M1, K1, M1, knit to the end of the round. (See pages 15 and 16 for how to M1.) *You now have* 22 stitches.

ROUNDS 4, 6, AND 8: Knit to the end of each round.

ROUND 5: M1, K3, M1, knit to the end of the round.
You now have 24 stitches.

ROUND 7: M1, K5, M1, knit to the end of the round.
You now have 26 stitches.

ROUND 9: Slip the first 7 stitches (thumb stitches) onto a stitch holder, cast on 1 stitch, and knit to the end of the round.
You now have 20 stitches on the needles.

Knitting the Hand

ROUNDS 1–9: Knit to the end of each round.

ROUND 10: K1, K2tog, K5, ssk, K1, K2tog, K5, ssk.
You now have 16 stitches.

ROUNDS 11 AND 13: Knit to the end of each round.

ROUND 12: K1, K2tog, K3, ssk, K1, K2tog, K3, ssk.
You now have 12 stitches.

ROUND 14: K1, K2tog, K1, ssk, K1, K2tog, K1, ssk.
You now have 8 stitches.

Cut the yarn, thread the tail through the remaining stitches with a yarn needle, pull together, and fasten off.

Making the Thumb

SETUP: Slip the 7 stitches from the stitch holder onto two double-pointed needles. With the third needle, pick up 3 more stitches from the body of the mitt. *You now have* 10 stitches.

ROUNDS 1–5: Using MC, knit to the end of each round.

ROUND 6: *K2tog; repeat from * to the end of the round.
You now have 5 stitches. Cut yarn.

With a yarn needle, thread the yarn through the remaining stitches and pull together. Fasten off.

Finishing

Sew the short seam in the cuff. Weave in all loose ends on the wrong side of the work. Felt the ornaments as described in Felting, right).

Add hangers (see page 77 for suggestions). Decorate with buttons or embroidery as desired (see page 105 for decorative stitches).

FELTING

To protect your washer from excess lint, place the knitted ornaments in a zippered, fine-mesh bag. If you felt several ornaments at once, use a separate bag for each color. Avoid felting light and dark ornaments together, as there is always some dye and fiber washed out during the process. Adding a pair of blue jeans to the load will shorten agitation time.

Set the washer for hot water, low water level, and maximum agitation. Add a small amount of a mild detergent.

Check on the felting progress every 5 minutes. Each time you check, remove all the ornaments from the bag, pull them into shape, and check their size before continuing. Reset the washer to continue agitating until you are happy with the size. Do not let the washer drain and spin.

Remove the ornaments from the bags. Rinse them completely by hand, using a towel to remove as much water as possible.

Shape them and lay them out to air-dry. When they are completely dry, apply trim or embroidery, if desired.

Ski Sweater Ornaments

DESIGNED BY NANCY LINDBERG

Once you've made one of these charming little sweaters, you won't be able to resist making others. What a great way to use up yarn leftovers and try out different color combinations! There's little shaping and no armholes to deal with — just knit a large tube for the body and two smaller tubes for the arms, then assemble the parts when the knitting is completed.

FINISHED MEASUREMENTS

❅ 3½" wide at the chest, 8¾" wide wrist to wrist, and 3¾" long

YARN

Rowan Fine Tweed, 100% wool, sport weight, 0.88 oz (25 g)/88 yd (80 m) skeins

❅ **MC**   45 yds
   ((#1))   Hawes (rose, 362)
   ((#2))   Malham (dark gray, 366)
   ((#3))   Leyburn (gold, 383)

❅ **CC**   20 yds
   ((#1))   Buckden (light gray, SH364)
   ((#2))   Hawes (rose, 362)
   ((#3))   Richmond (green, 381)

NEEDLES

❅ One set of five US 3 (3.25 mm) double-pointed needles *or size you need to obtain correct gauge*

GAUGE

❅ 24 stitches = 4" on US 3 (3.25 mm) needles in stockinette stitch

OTHER SUPPLIES

❅ Stitch marker, yarn needle, pins, cording or doll clothes hanger for each sweater

ABBREVIATIONS	
CC	contrasting color
K	knit
MC	main color
P	purl

Knitting the Body

SETUP: Using MC and double-pointed needles, cast on 48 stitches. Distribute stitches evenly among four needles (12 stitches per needle), and join into a round, being careful not to twist the work. Place a stitch marker after the first stitch on Needle 1 to mark the beginning of the round.

NOTE: *When working charts in this section, always begin where indicated on line 1 at the bottom of the appropriate chart, and work from right to left. For more information about working with two colors, see The Joy of Color on page 19, and Getting Around on page 16.*

ROUNDS 1–3: Work in K1, P1 ribbing.

ROUND 4: Knit to the end of the round.

ROUNDS 5–13: Using CC and MC, knit each round as you follow the Tree chart, Snowflake chart, or Heart chart on page 130 for the color pattern. Repeat each pattern to the end of the round. Do not cut CC when you reach the end of the pattern.

ROUNDS 14–16: Using MC, knit to the end of the round.

ROUNDS 17–28: Using MC and CC, knit each round as you follow the Dot chart on page 130 for the color pattern. Repeat the pattern 12 times around. Complete lines 1–8, then repeat lines 1–4.

ROUNDS 29–31: Using MC and CC, knit each round as you follow the Zigzag chart on page 130 for the color pattern. Repeat the pattern 12 times around. Cut CC, leaving a tail to weave in later.

ROUND 32: Using MC, knit to the end of the round.

ROUNDS 33–35: Work in K1, P1 ribbing.

Bind off all stitches. (There is no armhole.)

Knitting the Sleeves (make 2)

SETUP: Using MC, cast on 18 stitches. Distribute the stitches evenly among three needles (6 stitches per needle) and join into a round, being careful not to twist the work. Place a stitch marker after the first stitch on Needle 1 to mark the beginning of the round.

ROUNDS 1–3: Work in K1, P1 ribbing.

ROUND 4: *K2, increase 1 in the next stitch by knitting into the front and then into the back of it; repeat from * to the end of the round.

You now have 24 stitches.

ROUNDS 5 AND 6: Knit to the end of the round.

ROUNDS 7–22: Using MC and CC, knit each round as you follow the Dot chart on page 130 for the color pattern. Repeat the pattern six times around. Work lines 1–8 twice (two vertical repeats).

ROUNDS 23–25: Using MC and CC, knit each round as you follow the Zigzag chart on page 130 for the color pattern. Repeat each pattern six times around. Cut MC.

Using CC, bind off all stitches.

Finishing

Turn the body and sleeves inside out and weave all loose ends into the wrong side of the work with a yarn needle.

Fold the sweater body with right sides together and the ending tail at one corner. Sew the shoulder seams by stitching just inside the bound-off stitches, working from the outside toward the center for 1" on each side. Turn the body and sleeves right side out.

Lay each sleeve on one side of the body with the yarn tail at the bottom and the bound-off edge just overlapping the side of sweater from the shoulder down. The bottom edge of each sleeve will be about 1¾" down from the shoulder. Pin; using the pattern yarn and a yarn needle, sew the sleeves in place, taking invisible stitches close to the bound-off edge, and allowing the bound-off stitches to form a decorative line around the false armhole.

Attach a cord to hang the sweater, or hang it from a doll clothes hanger.

TREE

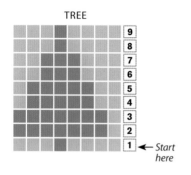

← *Start here*

SNOWFLAKE

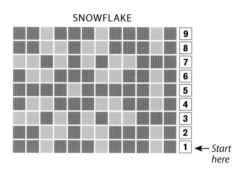

← *Start here*

HEART

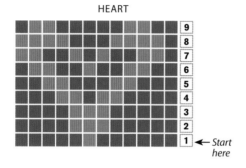

← *Start here*

DOT

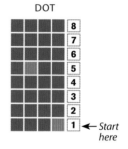

← *Start here*

KEY

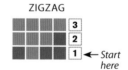

MC with Tree

MC with Snowflake

MC with Heart

CC with Tree

CC with Snowflake

CC with Heart

ZIGZAG

← *Start here*

Note: *If you are knitting the Snowflake or Heart pattern, use the same MC and CC colors that you've been using for the rest of the sweater, not those shown in the Dot and Zigzag charts.*

❋ CONTRIBUTING DESIGNERS ❋

EVELYN CLARK has been knitting off and on since she was eight. She is a freelance photographer, writer, and designer whose knitting patterns have been published by Fiber Trends, *Knitter's, Leisure Arts, Interweave Knits,* and *Vogue Knitting* magazines. She enjoys exploring new stitch patterns, especially in lace. She also teaches beginning knitting to elementary school children. She lives in Seattle, Washington.

LINDA DANIELS owns and operates Northampton Wools, in Northampton, Massachusetts, a full-service retail store offering knitting classes and a wide selection of yarns from around the world. *Interweave Knits* has featured many of her patterns, and she designed and knit several sweaters for the 1999 hit movie *The Cider House Rules.*

BEVERLY GALESKAS was owner and founder of Fiber Trends Pattern Company.

Canadian sisters Deb and LYNDA GEMMELL own and operate Cabin Fever, a hand-knitting pattern publisher, in Woodville, Ontario, Canada. The innovative duo design dozens of patterns for sweaters, hats, socks, and other apparel that are sold in yarn shops across North America. Most are knit in the round and in one piece, with virtually no sewing required. Plus sizes are also a standard element of most of their patterns.

NANCY LINDBERG developed her teaching skills while owning a yarn shop in Minneapolis for over a decade. She moved on to pattern designing and continues to teach, an activity that has garnered a large, faithful following. Her patterns appeal to all knitting levels and are available in yarn shops nationwide.

Retired from a successful corporate career, BETSY LEE MCCARTHY now enjoys designing simple, innovative knitwear patterns and teaching nationally and locally. Her sock and hat patterns have been published by Fiber Trends. Her *Knit Socks!,* first published in 2004, was released in a paperback version in 2011. She lives in Vancouver, Washington.

Owner of Sakonnet Purls, in Tiverton, Rhode Island, LOUISE SILVERMAN found the need to create patterns that take the mystery out of knitting. She calls her designs "Friendly Patterns for the Average Knitter." More than 40 Designs by Louise patterns are available in knitting and needlework stores nationwide.

BARBARA TELFORD'S Woodsmoke Woolworks is a farm-based knitwear and design shop based in Upper Gagetown, New Brunswick, Canada. She won the New Brunswick Craft Council's Oudemans Christmas Choice Award in 2002 for the ingenuity of her knitted hat collection. Her unique work is outstanding for her ability to produce witty and lively designs.

ACKNOWLEDGMENTS

Many thanks to the knitters and test knitters who helped make the projects for this book: Diana Foster, Barbara Kreuter, Kristy Lucas, Mary Ann Burch Nobben, and Claudia Wittman.

Index

Other Storey Titles You Will Enjoy

2-at-a-Time Socks, *by Melissa Morgan-Oakes.*

An easy-to-learn new technique to banish Second Sock Syndrome forever!
144 pages. Hardcover with concealed wire-o. ISBN 978-1-58017-691-0.

Knit Socks!, *by Betsy Lee McCarthy.*

Classic patterns for cozy feet — 17 patterns, plus valuable advice on
using alternative yarns and adapting patterns to any type of needle.
176 pages. Paper. ISBN 978-1-60342-549-0.

Knit Your Socks on Straight, *by Alice Curtis.*

Step-by-step visual instructions and 20 unique patterns to
create beautiful, comfortable socks — on straight needles.
144 pages. Hardcover with concealed wire-o. ISBN 978-1-61212-008-9.

The Knitter's Life List, *by Gwen W. Steege.*

A road map to a lifetime of knitting challenges and adventures.
320 pages. Paper with flaps. ISBN 978-1-60342-996-2.

The Knitting Answer Book, *by Margaret Radcliffe.*

Answers for every knitting quandary — an indispensable
addition to every knitter's project bag.
400 pages. Flexibind. ISBN 978-1-58017-599-9.

Sock Yarn One-Skein Wonders, *edited by Judith Durant.*

One-of-a-kind patterns for baby clothes, mittens,
scarves, hats, bags, and of course, socks!
288 pages. Paper. ISBN 978-1-60342-579-7.

These and other books from Storey Publishing are available
wherever quality books are sold or by calling 1-800-441-5700.
Visit us at *www.storey.com* or sign up for our newsletter
at *www.storey.com/signup.*